WHAT BLACKS DID NOT EXIST?

FELIX T. EHUI

African American IMAGES

CHICAGO, ILLINOIS

CONTENTS

DEDICATION

To the memory of my great-grandfather, King Ngaza I, and my grandfather, King Tano Allou, who in spite of Europeans' attempts to assimilate Black people into their own culture, struggled to safeguard African traditions and values.

To the memory of my grandmother, Kassy Ngo Antoinette, my mother, Kadio N'goran Agnes; my sister, Anne-Marie Affoua; and my brother, Prosper Ehui. They all died without knowing the truth and believed that Whites are superior to Blacks.

To my father, Pascal Ehui, who taught me that "no matter how long a piece of wood remains in the river, it never becomes a crocodile." He meant that I should never forget my African traditions and values even though I was learning Western culture.

To my daughter, Sonia-Larissa Ehui, and my son, Steven J.G. Pascal Ehui. I hope that they will grow to be proud of their race and their African traditions and values.

To all Black youth who may still believe that their ancestors did not contribute to the progress of the world and still feel inferior to other youth. I hope this book helps them to become proud of what and who they are so that they can contribute to the emancipation of our people.

ACKNOWLEDGMENTS

My special thanks . . .
To God for giving me health. He gave me inspiration, courage and strength to write this book. To the members of my family, especially, my brothers, Jérôme Ehui and Raphael Ehui; my sister, Thérèse Akouman; my uncle, Raphael Kadihaud; my cousin, Genevieve; my niece, Marie-Berthe; and Chantal-Eveline for their support when I was researching and writing this book.

To the Augustus sisters, Brenda and Paulette, for their criticism and editing of the English version of this book. To all the people who helped me to obtain the necessary information to write this book, especially Reverend Willie Wilson, Union Temple Baptist Church in Southeast, Washington, D.C.; Myra Eldridge, Bruce Harris, Professor Jesse McDade, and the experts at the World Bank in Washington, D.C.

FOREWORD

It is a distinct honor to comment on this significant effort of Mr. Felix T. Ehui. Too few persons have a meaningful grasp of the responsibility of a serious scholar to be helpful to the initiate. Mr. Ehui brings all the historical information in contemporary research but he never loses the focus of authentic origins. *What if Blacks did not exist?* Mr. Ehui raises a relevant and complex question which requires a multifaceted answer. If Blacks did not exist, there would not be any "Whites." That in itself would not be problematic. A few decades ago a play was written entitled "Day of Absence." It is a story that could take place anywhere in the U.S.A. where the Caucasian population is consciously and subconsciously dependent upon persons of Africa ancestry to perform menial and routine tasks. One day, the Blacks decide to "disappear." Needless to say, the Caucasians are very alarmed, worried, and depressed. They pray for the return of the Blacks.

This book raises substantive questions about the repercussions of this "absence." What would happen if Blacks did not exist? Are we expendable or indispensable? It logically follows that if Whites come from Blacks then there wouldn't be, nay, couldn't be a "White existence." Contrary to the prevailing ideology, White existence is biologically dependent upon Black people, so are their systems, science, and religious beliefs. Read Mr. Ehui's work with an open mind and ponder what for many Caucasians, is the inconceivable. The purpose of this exercise is to read what you think and see but cannot say.

Jesse McDade, Ph.D.
Professor of Philosophy
Maryland State University

If Blacks did not exist . . .

- America would not be the richest country in the world. They became rich because they had free labor from 1619-1865.

- There would be major traffic jams without the traffic light developed by Garrett Morgan.

- Medicine would not have its father and cataract surgery (Imhotep), blood plasma (Charles Drew), or open-heart surgery by Daniel Hale Williams.

- We would not believe in one God.

- We would be late without the lunar and solar calendar or the first clock.

- The NBA, NFL, and most sports would be very boring.

- Music would sound very strange.

- U.S. corporations would lose money because we spend 97 percent of our income with them.

- Then no other race would exist.

Dr. Jawanza Kunjufu
Publisher

INTRODUCTION

Using a comparative study of American and other cultures as a framework, I used to ask my students to draw their family trees and comment on them in front of the class. I noticed that Caucasian and Asian students drew family trees with more branches and deeper roots than African American students. I also noticed that African American students looked embarrassed when they were called on to talk about their ancestors. They did not seem to know much about them (or maybe they were ashamed).

One day, one of my African American students stood up and told me he was not going to say anything about his ancestors. When asked why, he responded that his ancestors were not worthy of discussion. Other groups reacted differently. They were proud of their ancestry because their understanding of self was not negative, nor were they "educated" to believe that they were "savages."

After this shocking conversation, I went to the head of the school and asked him to implement a Black history and culture course. He honored my request; unfortunately, there were few adequate textbooks on the subject. I could not help because I did not know much myself.

"Not to know is bad, but to refuse to know is worse."
A Gambian proverb (West Africa)

I decided to search for myself and eventually to write a book. It all started with the chapter about the family tree, I made a promise to myself to learn as much as I could about the origins of the world's races. The more I learn about Black people and their history, the more I realize I did not know, and the more I learn about myself. Every reading, every discovery

I make leads me to conclude that the history of Black people is the beginning point of the history of all other people. For example, if Blacks did not exist, no other races would have existed, for Blacks are the ancestors of all peoples.

For centuries, Caucasian scholars, historians, and writers have denied the contribution of Black people to world progress. In 1957, P. Gaxote wrote in *La Revue de Paris*, "These people (if you see who I mean) did not contribute anything to the progress of the world. Something may have happened that prevented them from doing so. They have nothing to their credit. They boasted no Euclid, no Aristotle, no Galileo, no Lavoisier, no Pasteur; they had no Homer to sing their eras."[1]

This mindset has served to justify slavery and colonization and to impose the European civilization upon Black people, to dominate and oppress them. Even today, the minds of many Black people are still not free of this yoke. Asa Hilliard comments:

> "Mental bondage is invisible violence. It is worse than physical slavery alone. We are told in the Western world that the Western civilization is the independent product of Western genius, that the rest of the world waited in the darkness until Western Europe brought the light. This fable has served to support slavery, racism, and oppression. When an occasional scholar, or member of the general public discovers new treatments of information that challenges the bedrock of the belief and thinking systems, that person is frequently met with silence, denial, isolation, even death."[2]

How can Black people be persuaded to believe that some of the things they have been taught are not historically true? Will it be easy for people to accept that the original Jews, including Abraham, Jacob, and Moses, were all Black? How can the many Black Christians in the world be persuaded to believe that Jesus was Black? These Christians have been told all their lives that Jesus Christ was a White person, and their minds are conditioned to believe what they were taught. How can one convince them to consider a different version and a different interpretation of the Bible? How can we make Black people understand that our salvation does not depend on Caucasians?

This book explains that Black people, contrary to what we have always been taught, were present everywhere, at all levels, sometimes voluntarily, sometimes against their own will, in building the world. If Blacks didn't exist, the world would not have been as great as it is today, for people of African descent forged the first civilization in the history of the world and contributed (in one way or another) to the development of Greek and Roman civilizations in antiquity. Black people saved Christianity from being annihilated. They laid the foundation of Western civilization.

Many of the arguments in this book lean on the fact that the ancient Egyptians were Black. Unfortunately, today because modern inhabitants of Egypt are of the Caucasian type, many Black people, especially Black Africans believe that the population of ancient Egypt was White. This confusion was created by Caucasian scholars and writers who have always presented the ancient Egyptian civilization as Caucasian. Other Caucasian scholars, such as Mary Lefkowitz, try to show that the population living in ancient North Africa was ethnically diverse.[3] However, the most important question is not, who was living in Egypt after it had become a great empire? but who forged Egypt at the beginning, and who made it become so great?

Before proceeding, it is essential to establish the blackness of ancient Egyptians. This fact was confirmed by Herodotus, "the Greek father of history," after he visited the Egyptian empire. He wrote, "They have burnt skin, flat noses, thick lips, and woolly hair."[4] Also, Karl Richards Lepsius, a German scholar, expressed surprise: "Where we expected to see an Egyptian, we are presented with an authentic Negro."[5]

Unlike Mary Lefkowitz who fails to prove the Caucasian origins of Egyptian civilization, many African scholars, including Cheikh Anta Diop and Ki Zerbo, have proved, with a great amount of historical data and archaeological artifacts, how the Nile Valley attracted Black Africans. Ki Zerbo notes:

> "During the fourth millennium BC, the Nile Valley witnessed a multiform and prodigious development of the populations who forged the first civilization in history: the civilization of Egypt of the Pharaohs. Far from being a miracle, the Egyptian civilization was the crowning of the leadership that Africa maintained over the first 3,000 centuries in human history."[6]

Egypt started growing around 3500 BC as cultures formed and economic and political strategies began to take shape. The Nile River drew from as far as the Sahara. The Nile, which had offered few interests, became an important settlement. Chiefs, priests, and their servants, started to specialize in different sectors of activities. A new, diversified, and complex society sprang out of the fertile Nile River. It was a mature, powerful, and originally organized group that emerged from the obscurities of prehistory."[7]

Pharaohs from the third dynasty, according to Pétrie and Ki Zerbo, were all Sudanese Blacks. They were authentic Negroes. "Pharaohs of the third dynasty were Sudanese. Ramses III looked Nubian, so was Amenhemat, first founder of the twelfth Egyptian dynasty. His mother was Nubian."[8]

In regards to the above information, it is more likely that people who migrated along the Nile Valley and created the original Egyptian civilization were people living in the geographic space of modern Egypt, Ethiopia, Chad, Central-African Republic, Sudan, Uganda, and Kenya.

Although the fall of ancient Egypt eventually forced Black Africans to move to the Southern, Eastern, and Western parts of Africa, they left behind traces of their great civilization all throughout the ancient Mediterranean zone.[9] Similarities between the Akan ethnic groups in West Africa and the ancient Egyptians can be found in the present day culture and philosophy of the former. The emblem of the Egyptian army is the same as the one of the Mani-Kongo, name of the king in the precolonial kingdom of Congo (Zaire). It was an idol, built on spikes, in the form of a Black general holding a sword. The burial vaults of the Agni ethnic group (Ivory Coast) look like those of the Nile Valley.

Black people started progressively and massively to move en masse into the Western, Southern, and Eastern parts of the African continent at the end of the second, third, and the beginning of the fourth centuries A.D. (after Jesus Christ's death).[10] Arabs did not begin to occupy Northern Africa until 639 A.D.[11]

In writing this book, I did not seek to prove that Blacks are superior or inferior to other cultural groups or races. My wish is for my Black sisters and brothers, and anyone else who wants to know more about Black people, to read this book objectively so they can discover truths that have been long hidden from the entire world. This will help them to reconsider what Caucasian writers and scholars have written about Black people.

The contributors to the original African Heritage Study Bible indicate:

> *"The role of Black history is not to prove that the contributions of Black people to world civilization are better or worse than other races, but to stress the simple fact that Africans and African descendants can look back upon their past with pride, for men and women of Black skin have contributed significantly to human progress."*[12]

Knowing our history has an ultimate purpose: freedom and emancipation. We cannot be free unless we are fully aware of who we are. This requires a clear awareness and a complete understanding of ourselves, our history, our people, and our race. We bury ourselves twice in misery if we learn the history of our people through the point of view of our oppressors. No one can teach us about ourselves better than ourselves.

Therefore, the first part of this book tries to reestablish a number of truths that have been intentionally and maliciously distorted. Black people have been so belittled that our children and our children's children believe that their ancestors were useless and Caucasians' history, intelligence, and civilizations are uncontaminated and universal.

Through the knowledge of our history, we can improve ourselves, respect ourselves, and cause other people to respect us. We must strengthen our will to fight for emancipation so that we can enjoy the benefits of freedom. We can become what we want to become. Our strength and richness will come from our unity.

In the second part of this book, I offer some strategies that are designed to strengthen our spiritual, economic and political status, cultural expressions and unity. We must first be aware of our people's pain, suffering, and distress. Then, we must unite as a big and strong family and work together to rebuild our communities. Without unity, all of our efforts, complaints, and calls for justice will be worthless, empty words. Without unity, we can be divided. If we are divided, we are fragile.

PART ONE

LIES AND TRUTHS

ABOUT BLACK PEOPLE

"History is man, always man and his admirable efforts. The history of Black people, if it is sincere and straight, can unfold into all men, into all people, into the whole world."[13]

THE FIRST EUROPEANS WERE BLACK

For many people, the White race is superior, and the other races are inferior. Among those subordinated races is the Black race that, according to White Christians, was cursed by Noah in the Bible.[14]

This doctrine that represents Blacks as cursed people and inferior beings was even supported by great European intellectuals, like Voltaire and Montesquieu. When asked if Europeans were originally Black, Voltaire said, "Only a blind person could believe such nonsense. The round in the eyes of the Negroes; their flat noses; their thick lips; their ears of a different form; the fur on their heads; and the feeble measures of their intelligence, put them between themselves and other prodigious species."[15]

Montesquieu, one of the greatest French lawyers and philosophers of the eighteenth century, expressed his opinion of Black inferiority this way, "These creatures have black all over their bodies and with their flat noses, what a pity! It is hard to believe that God who is a wise being could have put a soul, especially a good soul, in such a black and ugly body."[16]

Even today, at the end of the twentieth century, many White scholars continue to believe that Whites are more intelligent than Blacks. In the book *The Bell Curve: Intelligence and Class Structure in American Life,* Richard J. Herrnstein and Charles Murray skew a mountain of statistical "evidence" to "prove" that Blacks are intellectually inferior to Whites. The authors believe that intelligence is innate, not an artificial or social construct. They say that intelligence test scores diverge according to races and ethnic groups and that in the

United States, Blacks score 15 points lower than Whites. The authors argue that intelligence is strongly influenced by the genes of one's ancestors. Thus, Blacks will remain eternally less intelligent than Whites no matter their social and financial conditions and educational opportunities.[17]

What the authors of *The Bell Curve* overlooked is that the first human beings on earth were Black, and that White people descended from Blacks. If intelligence is influenced by the genes of one's forebears and if the first Europeans were Black, then White people's intelligence was transmitted by their Black ancestors. Following the reasoning of Herrnstein and Murray, we could conclude that intelligence was with Black people in the beginning. In other words, White people's intelligence depends upon Blacks. If Whites are intelligent, it is because Blacks transmitted it to them. If Blacks are not intelligent then neither are Whites.

Scientists and researchers such as Dr. Cheikh Anta Diop, Dr. Louis Leakey, Dr. Joseph Ki Zerbo, and George G. M. James have proven that Africa is the birthplace of mankind. They have proven that the first human being was Black and appeared in Africa, near the equator, at the Omo-Valley, the region where Tanzania is located today. Therefore, we will not waste time writing and arguing about a thesis that has already been unanimously accepted by researchers, anthropologists, archaeologists, historians, and geographers of all races: Whites, Yellows, and Blacks.

Diop elaborates:

"All the other races derive from the Black race by a more or less direct affiliation and the other continents were populated at the Homo erectus and Homo sapiens stages. The old theories that used to state that Blacks came from somewhere else are now invalid."[18]

Even the biblical creation story agrees that the first humans created by God, Adam first, and then Eve, were both put in the Garden of Eden, located in the eastern portion of Africa, where Sudan and Ethiopia are located today. So far, no historian, no archaeologist, and no religion have yet demonstrated that the first human being has not originated from Africa or was not Black.

No theologian has proven that God created two groups of people: one in Africa and the other somewhere else. Scientifically, archaeologically, and historically, all the research comes to the same conclusion: Africa is the cradle of mankind. From Africa, the rest of the world was populated.

According to Cheikh Anta Diop, the first Blacks who migrated to other parts of the world travelled through the Straight of Gilbratar, the Suez Canal, and through Sicily and Southern Italy. It has been proven through archaeological artifacts that the first known inhabitant of Europe was the Grimaldi man, a Black immigrant. His skeleton was discovered in France near Monaco. The late French professor and author, Raymond Vaufrey, decreed that at the time Blacks arrived in Europe, the continent was already populated. Paradoxically, Vaufrey did not prove that the first Europeans were White. Nor disprove that the first Europeans were Black.

Grimaldi man and even combe-capelle man (who had woolly hair) were the first Europeans. For modern Europeans to admit that their ancestors were Black is, perhaps, shameful. In their minds they are brought down to a primitive level, the same level to which they relegate Black people. Nevertheless, the findings of Cheikh Anta Diop have been confirmed by most historians and archaeologists. Among those is Joseph Ki Zerbo who wrote, *"Europe was invaded from Africa by a new type of human beings. It was in Europe, in Grimaldi, next to Monaco that the oldest skeletons of Homo sapiens, which were Negroids, were found."*[19]

How did the Black man become White in Europe? Why didn't the White man inherit the biological traits of his Black ancestor? Ki Zerbo answers this question. "With the diversification of climatic conditions and lifestyle, a slow differentiation has occurred. That is, a prolonged stay in a cold area, with veiled sunshine may have contributed to lighten the color of the skin, slimmer the nose, increase the pilosity and the adiposity that help resist the climate; whereas adaptation to heat and tropical humidity increased dark pigmentation, enlargement of the nostrils, richness of sudoriferous glands, and the glabrous character of the skin. Melanin and woolly hair protect from the heat."[20]

Racial differentiations started in Europe, in Southern France and in Spain, about 20,000 years ago. Morphological studies have shown that the first White man appeared only 20,000 years ago: Cro-Magnon man. How did the Grimaldi man become White? According to Gloger's scientific theory which stipulates that skin pigmentation changes to adapt to climatic conditions. The Cro-Magnon man was the result of mutations from the Grimaldi Black man inside Europe for 20,000 years in the exceedingly cold climate due to the long glaciation in the low latitude mountainous regions.

Today, the Basques and Catalans, who live in the Franco-Cantabrian region where the Cro-Magnon man was born, are the descendants of the Cro-Magnon man. The inhabitants of Southern France (in the Midi region) and inhabitants of Spain and Italy have tanned mulatto skins; those living in the Northern regions have lighter skin.

If race does not count, why didn't Europeans use the indigenous people of America, the so-called Indians to work their farms? Why, in the United States, do some Whites reject some Black people's job applications with little regard to their qualifications or their education?

The truth has been distorted. Lies have survived the centuries. The lie made the world believe that the first European was a White man. The lie made the world believe that White people forged the first world civilization and that Black people were incompetent and had to be educated by White people. The truth is that the Black man is the ancestor of the White man and all other races. If Blacks did not exist, Whites, Reds, Yellows, and Brown would not exist.

WERE BLACKS SAVAGES BEFORE
THE SLAVE TRADE?

Many Caucasians try to make Black Americans believe that their African ancestors were savages before the slave trade occurred. They wanted to make Black Americans believe that if their ancestors had not been captured and enslaved in America, they would still be living like savages in Africa today. This lie continues to reinforce the ideology of White supremacy and Black inferiority.

Black scholars like Keith B. Richburg, a journalist who writes for the *Washington Post*, help to reinforce the lie. After a visit to Africa, Richburg wrote that the word "African" should not antecede the word "American" when referring to Black Americans because Africa as a whole is a shame.[21] Despite the horrors that our enslaved ancestors experienced, Richburg is grateful that we came to America. He believes that slavery was a blessing from God. He says that he feels cynical, jaded, bitter and largely devoid of hope, and drained of compassion -- a condition on which he blames Africa. Richburg lambastes Whites in the West who hesitate to hold Blacks, and Black Americans accountable for their own woes.[22]

Keith Richburg enjoys many opportunities his ancestors and contemporaries in Africa and America might only dream about. As the Washington Post's Africa Bureau chief, he has travelled all over the world. Apparently, he does not know or remember how humiliating it was for our Black ancestors to be treated as nothing, to be battered just because they spoke to a White person or replied to a White person's insult. Keith

Richburg does not seem to remember how painful it was to be unjustly charged and punished for crimes whose only "evidence" was skin color. He does not seem to know any thing about the history of his Black American ancestry, the history of Black people in America. For centuries, Caucasian historians and writers have denied that the African continent had a history and civilizations. In 1830, Hegel, a German philosopher declared:

> "Africa is not a historic part of the world. It can show no developments or internal historic movements. Its northern part belongs to the Asian or European world. Our perception of Africa is precisely an undeveloped spirit, still wrapped in natural conditions, and to be hereto presented only as on the threshold of world history."[23]

However, authentic scientific and historical data gathered by historians and researchers such as Cheikh Anta Diop, Joseph Ki Zerbo, Jean Suret Canal, Dr. Louis Leakey, Walter Rodney, and others verify the existence of a real African history. These researchers approach the study of Africa with more rigor, objectivity, and open-mindedness. To achieve this they use primary and secondary documents and artifacts from Africa and other parts of the world.

It remains an undisputed fact that Africa was present in the Neolithic Age and in antiquity. Three thousand years before Christ, Black Egyptians invented the calendar of 365 $\frac{1}{4}$ days. They also developed the first script in the history of the world. Later on, 500 years before Jesus Christ's birth, iron was discovered in Nubia where modern Ethiopia is located. Great empires such as Ghana, Mali, and Songhaï flourished during the Middle ages. Furthermore, Blacks developed great universities, such as the universities at Sankore, Walata, Gao, and Timbuktu, long before the slave trade and the European colonialism.

Nevertheless, for most Westerners, Africa has always been the land of "primitive" people and "savages." In 1875, Henry

Morton, an American journalist, was sent to Africa by the *New York Herald*, under the cover of the British government. He was sent to look for lands to colonize. About the Blacks he wrote, "These savages, they only respect force."[24] Europeans used this argument in part to justify colonialism.

Even today, many Westerners see Africa as the land of implacable sun and grass huts. If you mention the skyscrapers of Abidjan, Lagos, Yaoundé, Accra, Nairobi, Libreville, or Dakar, you will arouse surprise. It is time to stop dreaming. Africa has a glorious history, an incomparable richness of cultures, and great social values. It is time to stop the stereotypes passed down for generations and encouraged by the Western media. The time has come to broaden our horizons and embrace the whole spectrum of world history and cultures. Values that are not Western are not necessarily bad or savage because there is no universal chart of values.[25] Africa was not a continent inhabited by "savages" before the slave trade and colonization. Blacks had their writing and their political, economic, and social organization.

A Roman adage says that to function, every community needs rules that govern the relationships between its members. Violation of these rules results in sanctions. "Ubis societas, ibi jus" means "Wherever there is a society, there is a law." As Yves Brillon says, "There can be no collective if discipline and order are not imposed on its members."[26] To understand the regulation system in the pre-colonial African societies, we must first understand the philosophy of the organization and the functioning of power in these societies. This can only be possible if we envision the political organization and its functioning according to a classification based on cultural and structural affiliations.

Before the slave trade and colonialism, Africa was culturally and politically, composed of two major groups: monarchies and clans. In African monarchies, the king was the absolute ruler, and was often deified. In some regions, it was forbidden to say the name of the king or even his title. No one could say "I am going to the king. Instead, they would say, "I am going to the power." The king was always approached with an attitude of humbleness.

The authority of the king was tapered off by the presence of an advisory council. The king consulted the council on important subjects. The council expressed its opinion, but the final decision was made by the king in the name of the throne. Council members were chosen from a list of dignitaries who each specialized in different functions of the administration. Their roles were similar to ministers or secretaries in the Western societies today.

Some kingdoms were as large as the states of Illinois, Indiana, or Arkansas. These large kingdoms were divided into districts; the districts were divided into villages; and villages were divided into households. In big kingdoms like the kingdoms of Benin, Yoruba, Congo, Abron, Agni, and Ashanti, there was a prime minister. Depending on the kingdom, he was elected for three or five-year terms. He could be reelected indefinitely. The prime minister was nominated by the king. His appointed was confirmed by the council.

The prime minister's cabinet was comprised of the following positions:

1. Minister of Internal Affairs: he was responsible for the social and cultural harmony between the different districts chiefs and the king; He was also responsible for the economic and social activities such as constructing or repairing the roads between two districts;

2. Minister of Communication: he coordinated the relation ships between the royal palace, institutions, and the people;

3. Minister of Defense and War: he had three responsibilities: he was in charge of the protection of the kingdom

against foreign aggressions. His second responsibility was to lead the army in case of a war. He was the chief of staff of defense. Finally, he was the chief of the secret services of the king. He had at least one secret agent in each of the neighboring kingdoms. These secret agents informed him of any possible foreign aggression or any machination from another king;

4. Royal Consul: he coordinated the diplomatic relationships between the king and the neighboring kingdoms;

5. Minister of Finance: he managed the king's wealth. This function was equivalent to the Minister of Treasury or Finance in Western countries today.

Unlike the kingdoms, pre-colonial African clans were sometimes as small as 50 to 100 people. The power of the chief was limited to the small geographic space of the village. Compared to the power of the king, the power of the clan chief was almost insignificant. Because of the sizes of the pre-colonial African clans, it was very easy for the European colonialists to conquer them. White people even used them in their armies to conquer the kingdoms.

European colonialists wrote that the African clans had no form of organized power because most of the times, the clan chief who was the strongest (physically) person in the clan abused his power. Other times it was the magician or the witch doctor who was the abusive chief. These individuals usually usurped the power by force and they took advantage materially and emotionally of the other inhabitants of the clan.

However, in normal circumstances, the political organization and functioning in the clans were an early form of democracy. Unlike the monarchies in which the succession of the king was hereditary, in the clans, the seat of power did not hold a lifetime guarantee. Elections were held so that the people could choose their political representatives.

The representatives were elected for terms of three to five years (depending on the clans) and they could be reelected for as long as the people wanted them. If a representative died before the expiration of his mandate, elections were held immediately following the funeral.

In their attempt to analyze the system of production in pre-colonial Black Africa, many people have theorized that pre-colonial Blacks were Communists. These people's mistake is to believe that solidarity means communism. In a Communist system, all the possessions belong to the state for whom all the citizens work. The citizens do not have the right and freedom to create their own businesses. The private sector does not exist. This was not true in pre-colonial Black Africa. The land belonged to all the people living in the clan or the kingdom. Everybody had the right to exploit the values of the land. A wealthy person could grant himself the services of employees and compensate them materially or financially. Clan chiefs and the king intervened in the economic system only to arbitrate conflicts between two and more families. The second mistake is to confuse family business and communism. Members of African families used to associate to do business together. Blacks were never dissociated from their families. If an individual was wealthy, his whole family was seen as wealthy as well.

The search for material wealth in the context of family business was very ingrained into the Black Africans' mentality. It was so developed in Black African societies that people invented all kinds of institutions and systems. Being wealthy was a real competition among families. This competition was a ground for the institution of polygamy.

A man who had no children had very little chances to become wealthy, because children were an important workforce. A man who had many wives was more likely to have many children; consequently, if he had many children, he had many "employees" and therefore he had substantial chances of being wealthy. Sterility was very badly perceived by Blacks because a woman who could not procreate could bring no material aide to her husband and to her family. Family was therefore an important core in the system of production. It was an element so important that Blacks never abandoned a parent who had some financial difficulties. Combined with solidarity and cooperation among the members of the same age group, free enterprise and free trade were the key elements of the production system in pre-colonial Black Africa. Task division was based on sex, age, and education. Each developmental stage had its own learning programs and test. With the passage of each stage came new levels of self-discovery and maturity. The socialization process was designed to integrate each individual into the life of the community.

Age and birthright were the foundation of the economic and social systems, which were established before the slave trade and colonialism.

. 6 to 12 years old: Children learned to tell stories through the fairy tales and legends, and songs of their ethnic group. They learned arithmetic (counting). Boys learned the names of animals and developed their hunting skills. Some of them learned how to fish. They followed their parents and big brothers and watched them as they farmed or made examples. By hunting together, children in this age group learned how to socialize and collaborate. They learned to treat each other like brothers. By eating and hunting together, they learned to share and to look after each other. Most important is, as they fought together for the same cause, they learned that team work gets the best results.

The girls in this age group baby-sat their younger brothers and sisters. Girls are taught at an early age that children are the reward of life.[27] They learned how to cook and they gathered water and firewood. The home is the central place for the family and women are charged with this major responsibility.[28] By watching everything the older women did, they already learned how to be a woman and to be good housekeepers.

. 13 to 18 years old: The teenagers in this age group entered a more serious phase of their lives. They learned the history of their ethnic group, village and lineage. They learned the names of all the neighboring villages and the relationships between those villages and their own. They learned mental calculation, agriculture, fishing, and advanced hunting techniques. The teenagers had to master war, fighting, and wrestling techniques. They learned proverbs and parables which were considered to be the secrets of communication. Most importantly, they were given more responsibilities in the community, such as the education of children and management of the land. They were learning to be spouses and parents.

Sometimes marriages were arranged. For example, in the Akan ethnic groups, it was an obligation for the father to find good wives for his boys. He had to take care of all the expenses for the wedding. After the wedding, it was still his responsibility to make sure that his sons treat their wives with respect and honor. So, from his sons' youngest ages, he had a view on a girl in the community. When the girl had grown up, he would propose to his son to marry her. If the son agreed, they will go together and ask for her hand in the name of the family. If after this first marriage, the son decided to have a second wife, he had to look for one himself and he had to pay for the expenses himself. In this last case, the marriage may not be arranged. There were other situations where the young people chose each other without their parent's involvement.

. 19 to 29 years old: Most of them were mothers already and were busy providing food for their families. In monarchical societies, women in this age group served as counselors in the women's committee and recommended potential candidates to the position of village chief. At this point, women knew the family trees of every family in the community. The main duty of the young men was to assure the protection of the community, as well as earn revenue for their families. They were taught leadership traits. This prepared them for their future responsibilities as potential counselors and ministers.

. **30 to 55 years old:** Those men and women in the previous age group who proved their leadership abilities wisdom were called to serve as administrators. Some of them were called to work with the district council or to serve as ministers or counselors in the royal administration. Women were the chief negotiators for arranged marriages and for choosing names for newborns. Some men became ministers, clan chiefs, and kings.

. **55 and upwards:** Men and women in this age group could retire from economic activities, but because of their social experience, they were often called to serve as judges at the village or regional courts (tribunal sessions that heard cases across many villages). Some of them were solicited to be notables during public assemblies. Women were charged with organizing wedding and customary ceremonies and religious rites and rituals.

Every man and woman who lived beyond the age of 70 had fully served his community and had to retire. He earned respect and honor. At this advanced age, men and women occasionally counselled the younger generations.

In Africa, no matter the type of political organization or ethnic group, the terms "aunt," "cousin," "stepfather," and "stepmother" do not exist. Every older person is considered a big sister or a big brother. However, if this older person is the same age as your parents, you must call him/her "father" or "mother" even if there is no biological relationship. Members of the same age set are "brothers" and "sisters." A friend of your big brother or big sister must be called "big brother" or "big sister." This explains the tight relationships and solidarity among members of the same community in Africa. It also explains why Africans from the same community help each other. Africans were not "savages" before they met European colonists. No savages can have such a structured organization.

No civilization could have existed without such highly defined social structures.

European mythology states that African civilizations are based solely on oral expression. They see Africa as a continent whose cultural drive has been expressed only through the spoken word. European scholars maintain that Blacks had no access to any cultures and histories prior to their indoctrination.

This assertion should be reconsidered. Researchers have discovered that writing was known in Africa; that many African societies had developed systems of writing to retain certain aspects of their underlying culture. Griaule and Dieticker found that the Bambaras[29] preserved their essential knowledge by means of a system of signs and *ideograms*. The Bamous of Cameroon, the Vai of Sierra Leone, and the Nsibidi of Eastern Nigeria, for example, had graphic signs. Genevieve Calme Griaule discovered the existence of a diagrammatic sign used by the Dogond of Mali and Guinea.[30] The Egyptians wrote in hieroglyphs over 6,000 years ago. Many Blacks societies developed their own writing systems before they met Europeans. But, why did they favor the spoken word over writing?

The spoken word has always occupied an important place in the lives of African people. For Africans, the universe is permeated with an active force which man controls through the mastery of the spoken word. Through the Word, life was created. Thus, for man to be in perfect harmony with God and the universe, he must attach the utmost priority to developing speech that draws on the power of the Word.

Thus, African writing systems often transmit special knowledge to be read by a small, elite cadre of enlightened persons. Writing is not to be popularized. Writing does not substitute the spoken word, but supports it. This African concept of writing is one outcome of one approach of the Black African dialectic and ontological visions of the world.

THE BLACK HOLOCAUST AND THE DECLINE OF THE BLACK RACE

How could the cradle of humanity and civilization, host continent to great empires of the Middle Ages, end up invaded, bought, and humiliated by European powers? Is Africa responsible for its underdevelopment? What stopped the development of Africa? The answer to these questions depends on the way one perceives Africa today and most of all, on the knowledge that one has of Black history.

Before the slave trade, Africa had very structured political and social systems. As in every society, there were social classes (upper, middle, and lower). Africa had leaders and followers as can be found in today's modern societies and had developed a commercial trade system. Like its Western counterparts, Africa has seen its share of ethnic wars. But these wars, unlike those started in Europe in 1914 and 1939, never turned into world wars.

Africa regarded mutual assistance as a high social value: all individuals from the same community came to each other's help. The problems faced by one member of the community were the concern of all those related to, or associated with the community. Suicide was almost nonexistent in Africa. When a baby was born, it was welcomed by the whole community. No mother would abandon or kill her child, claiming that the child was too cumbersome or too expensive for her to raise. She was confident that in times of great difficulty, the community would lend her a helping hand. Had African societies been left to evolve on their own terms, without any interference from European or Arab invaders, the continent could have been a world leader. Unfortunately, two phenomena greatly distorted the course of its history: the slave trade and colonialism.

A time-honored African cultural tradition consists of making a stranger feel welcome in the community. A stranger with no family ties is taken to the village chief, who will make it a priority to provide a shelter for him. Then he will be questioned about the purpose of the visit. Is this naiveté or trust? Blacks believe that nobody in their right mind would risk entering a village to start problems when they knew they were at such a physical disadvantage. During the stranger's stay, if he behaves well, he will receive all honors.

This is how the White man was welcomed by Blacks, with open arms. How did he handle this welcome? The first thing he did was to study and analyze the traditions, customs, and inter-ethnic relations (including ethnic wars and the capture of prisoners of war who were turned into slaves). Then, he began to implement a game plan to buy the conscience of the ethnic group chiefs through worthless presents appreciated, however, by some Blacks leaders.

The White man managed to persuade the village chiefs to give him war prisoners in exchange for junk instead of waiting for restitution from the conquered group. Thus, these village chiefs who knew nothing of Europe and America, sold fellow Blacks to the Europeans. Before these village chiefs realized the damage they were causing their own communities, things had already gotten out of control. Some barbarian Blacks associated with Europeans and made slave trade their businesses. These barbarians captured whoever they could capture and sold them to Europeans. Africa was drained of its people.

The kings and clan chiefs had no idea how White slave traders treated Blacks on the ships and the American plantations. The slaves were brought from inside the continent, picked up from all along the coast, stocked as if they were merchandise in a stinking warehouse called "barracons." Around those ominous ugly barracks, one could witness hellish scenes. In particular, one could see many babies separated from their mothers. Scrupulously, the traders operated a deep and complete anatomic scrutiny on the slaves. Blacks were sold by auction. From the beginning to the end of the trip, the slaves were lying, one body against another, sometimes in the position of a spoon. They were so huddled together that they were literally swimming in a fringe of blood, vomiting, and rejections of any kind. As the passage lasted two months, one can imagine the large extent of mortality and epidemic. It was frightful. No matter what the traders tried, the slaves fought back, sometimes even lynching the traders. Most often, however, these revolts were quickly drowned in blood, sometimes with a hail of bullets. The leaders of the revolts were immediately executed or thrown overboard. Some of them were whipped in front of everybody. Their buttocks were slashed with kitchen knives; the wounds were impacted with a mixture of pepper, vinegar and powder. The leaders of hunger strikes were killed on the upper deck, cut into pieces, cooked and served as a meal to the other slaves. Before the arrival, the slaves who were too sick to be sold, but for whom the owner still had to pay property taxes were thrown overboard.[31]

The extent of slavery is hard to estimate because the trade continued for several centuries. Africa was "bled white" by the European slave merchants. To date, nobody can give a correct measure of the real impact of this flat-out human bleeding on the future of the African continent, documents

Ibrahima Baba Kaké.[32] Two or three out of four Blacks died before the arrival in America. They died of hunger, thirst or because they could not withstand drinking the sea water. Those who died were fed to the sharks.

Léopold S. Senghor estimates that between 60 million and 100 million Black people lost their lives during the slave trade.[33] This is more than the number of people killed in the two world wars combined. The Black holocaust (Maafa) was the most devastating massacre of humanity to occur in recorded history.

Depleted of its human potential, Africa's thinkers, youth, and labor force could no longer grow at the same pace as other continents. Thus began the slow-down of the African continent. Further aggravating Africa's decline was colonization that occurred three and half centuries later. Today, more than 500 years later, Black Americans are still struggling for their cultural identity and for a place as human beings in the American society.

Was slavery abolished for humanitarian reasons? The second major encounter between Blacks and Europeans occurred in the second half of the nineteenth century, during the Industrial Revolution. During the first period, Africa gave away its populations to enrich both the merchant ship owners from Liverpool, London, Nantes, Bordeaux, Barcelona, Amsterdam, Anvers, and the European colonists in America. However, with the Industrial Revolution, raw materials were henceforth, the focus of Europe's interest in Africa.

Strangely enough, colonization coincides with the Industrial Revolution in Europe and the abolition of slavery. How is that? Europeans now needed Blacks to stay on the African soil to extract the raw materials needed to keep their industries going. African slaves were freed. Some of them were then repatriated to Africa. Thus, Monrovia in Liberia and

Freetown (Sierra Leone) were created. Severed from their cultural origins, they had to start from square one while the rest of the world was moving ahead.

Unlike the slavery period when many African kings and clan chiefs naively cooperated with Europeans, the colonization era was characterized by many resistances. This is illustrated by the great resistance of Samory Touré, Mohammed Idriss es-Sénoussi, and King Gbéanzin to name only a few. Unfortunately, however, the colonial powers reached their goals and Africa was divided into regions, with no consideration for the pre-existing ethnic or structural realities.[34] This dividing was so arbitrary that today, one can find Yorubas in Nigeria and Benin; Adjas in Togo and Benin; Minas in Togo, Ghana, and Benin; Senefou and Lobis in Ivory Coast and Burkina-Faso; Haoussa in Niger and Nigeria; Akan in Ivory Coast and Ghana; and Hutus and Tusis in Angola, Zaïre, Congo, Rwanda, and Burundi.

European scholars often say that Africa could have benefited from colonization. They cite the Japanese model to prove their point. The Japanese came into contact with Europeans at around the same time as Blacks, but the nature of contact differed greatly. Many people believe that Blacks could have chosen Western culture, the way the Japanese or the Koreans did. However, what they fail to take into account is the fact that neither the Japanese nor the Koreans experienced slavery under the West. Japan was never drained of its men and women. Furthermore, Japan did not have the same resources (in terms of raw materials) as Africa; thus Europeans did not have the same intentions when they went to Japan. Japan was not carved into small pieces. No new civilization, no new national language only spoken by a tiny part of the population were imposed upon the Japanese. No social or cultural structures were taken apart. The end results were bound to be different.

The great lie of the West is that Blacks are lazy and disorganized, thus they deserve to be treated the way they are being treated by Caucasians today. The truth is that slavery and colonization emptied Africa of its human and natural resources. Slavery and colonization enriched Europe and America. If Blacks had not participated in the slave trade and colonization, how might Europeans have managed their economies? How developed would Europe and the United States be today? Most certainly, they would not be as advanced as they are today, for the Black holocaust through slavery and colonization help to build Europe and America.

"Many in the 1990s who think of a Black Jesus as an oddity or scandalous distortion of historical facts insist that Jesus was Semitic, or Middle Eastern. However, to call Jesus Semitic does not take us very far, because this nineteenth-century term refers not to a racial type, but to a family of languages including both Hebrew and Ethiopic."[35]

WHAT COLOR WAS JESUS?

For many years now I have heard many people from different races and cultural groups arguing about the cultural and racial origin of Jesus. I have always tried my best to stay out of a discussion that involved God or the Son of God. The reason was that I had always thought that Jesus, should not be understood as having a color. Whatever Jesus skin color or cultural origin was not subject to debate. I never paid any attention to the cultural origins of the peoples in the Bible. I was taught well by White missionaries and preachers. Through their teaching, they had given me the impression that Christianity was a European import and that Jews, including Moses and Jesus, were all White. I believed them.

This was my philosophy until one day, at the Smithsonian Museum, in Washington, D.C., I met a Black man who told me he was Jewish. First, I did not believe him because his skin color was as dark as my own. Then, he told me all about the Falashas or "Black Jews" of Ethiopia. He also told me that I should be more careful when I am reading the Bible because there are more Blacks in the Bible than I could possibly imagine. He added that a religion is supposed to be based on moral values and the truth. Therefore, it is a shame for Caucasian Christians to mistakenly represent Jesus as a White being.

After that, I had to deal with three different situations that shook me out of my passivity. In the first incident, a Muslim friend, who wanted me to switch religions, told me that Islam is for Black people and Christianity is for Whites. The second incident was my watching of the movie *Jesus of Nazareth*. I noticed that the man who was playing Jesus was White and had blond hair, and blue eyes. In the third incident a Caucasian friend told me that Christianity was created by Europeans. In addition, he said, all Jews are White. Since Jesus was Jewish, he concluded that he must have been White. For the first time, I argued about Jesus' skin color. A Black African who was with us and seemed to support the Caucasian's position challenged me to prove that Jesus was not White. So, I promised them to search for the truth. This was not about racism, cultural pride, or Africentrism. It was about the Truth.

From the time Black people came to America until 1842, they were not allowed to be Christians. It was said that Blacks were animals, so they could not be Christians. In 1842, a European pastor, Reverend C. C. Jones said to the slaves' masters, "Let us let them be Christians because I have taken the Christian message and I have developed a brand of Christianity that will make them more submissive." So he laid it out in a manual called *Instruction for Negro Slaves in America*,[36] which was solely designed to maintain slavery.

Since slavery, there have always been two kinds of Christianities in America: the one that Europeans control and the one that tries to be true to its African roots. The whole European concept of religion entails a compartmentalization of religious, political, economic, and social spheres. The Black concept is one that does not separate these spheres. They all belong together as one life. However, the theology that was taught to Black people by Caucasians was neither empowering nor enlightening. For example, every slave had to repeat the following words: *I realize that as a slave, I should not expect to have anything here on earth, but when I die and go to Heaven, I would get my reward.*[37]

This statement was designed to prevent slaves from wanting to secure material possessions. Individual salvation was the main goal. That theology is still being taught to this day. The songs, the messages in many Black churches make people think that the less they have, the less they can do for themselves, and they are holier. So what Blacks were taught during slavery remains true to a large degree.

Christians all over the world have been taught that Jesus was White. In their teaching, Europeans missionaries have always given the impression that Christianity is a European import. They used Christianity to penetrate Africa and imposed that religion on African people, presenting a White Jesus and even a White God. Is this historically, culturally, anthropologically, geographically, and biblically true? What was the real cultural and racial origin of Jesus Christ?

Jesus was not White, even though in movies, such as *Jesus of Nazareth*, in books, and churches, from Europe to America, from Africa to the Middle East, we have seen and we can still see White representations of Jesus (with blue eyes), Mary, Joseph, and the Apostles. However, biblical evidence points to a Black Jesus Christ.

Names and words about the genealogy of Jesus prove that he was of African descent. For example, in Matthew, chapter 1, we are told about Jesus' ancestors, who were descendants of Canaan. Canaan was the son of Ham, and Ham was Black. Many people believe that Ham, son of Noah, was cursed into blackness and, therefore, all people who descended from him (the Black race) were cursed. However, a deeper study of the Bible shows that the curse was not placed on Ham. The

Bible says that the curse was placed upon Canaan who was the son of Ham (Genesis 9:25). Why would Noah curse Canaan who was his grandson instead of his son, Ham, who saw him (Noah) naked and did not cover him? (Genesis 9:20-24).

We know that the first human on earth was Black. Nothing so far has proven that from Adam to Noah, there was a change of skin color. As Noah was from Adam and Eve's lineage, he could be nothing but Black. Nothing in the Bible shows that Noah and his three sons became White or Yellow after they spent 119 days on the ark. The Bible does not teach us that they became different from what they were before entering the boat. Noah and his sons were all Black when they entered the boat, and they came out of it with the same skin color. The alleged curse on Canaan, son of Ham, did not happen during the flood while they were inside the boat. Canaan was not in the boat with Noah. The alleged curse happened after they got out (Genesis 8 and 9). If Noah and his sons were Black, how could Ham, (or his son Canaan) who was already Black, become Black after he was cursed by Noah? If he was really cursed, there is no way he could have become Black. If that curse really happened, if any person was cursed, then that person became another color other than Black.

Ancient Egyptians and Ethiopians had a different version of the curse. They believed that the curse occurred, but the change of color was from Black to White and the curse was placed upon Cain after he killed Abel, his brother. This explains why ancient Egyptians and Ethiopians represented God as a Black being and the devil as a White being. Author and historian W. Reade says that originally all human beings were Black, but when God became angry with Cain for killing Abel, his brother, he yelled at Cain, and his skin color changed from Black to White. Thereafter, Cain's skin could no longer tolerate the heat. He could no longer plow the soil. That was his punishment.[38] If this is true, we could understand why White people's skins get easily burnt by the sun, even when they are simply trying to get a tan. Maybe that is also why they cannot do as well as Blacks when it comes to working or playing under the sun or when it is hot. God punished Cain (and through Cain, all White people) by reducing the melanin level in his body. **Note:** About the change of color from Black to White, please, read also the Bible (2 Kings 5:15-27).

In the books of Daniel and Revelation, Jesus is described with hair the texture of wool and feet the color of bronze. When King Herod wanted to kill Jesus, Joseph hid him in Egypt. Can a White man during that era be hidden in Egypt?

Many people say that it does not matter the color of Jesus; that we should worship Him in spirit and truth. I agree. But why do so many people choose to portray an image which happens to be White and erroneous? For that reason, I believe that Jesus' color matters very much. Many people think that God is White, and so is Jesus. They think that the people in the Bible must have been White. So many people of African descent look at White people almost as gods. All of this has to do with the way Christianity has been taught. In many churches attended by Black people in America and even in Africa, for example, one can see large pictures of a White Jesus. This has an effect on how people envision Jesus and God. In their prayers, they think of a White Jesus.

Black people will be saved if they know the truth. How can Black people know the truth when it has been twisted and distorted by Europeans to make us say what they want, do what they want, and think the way they want us to think? We have not been given the true message of Christ. His message was clear: he came for the oppressed, the poor, the imprisoned, and the brokenhearted (Luke 4:18-19).

Jesus was born at a time when ancient Egypt had been invaded by White people, at a time when the truth about the Egyptian civilization and its wonders was to becoming distorted as a Greek and Roman creation. Jesus was born at a time when Blacks were being massacred by Greeks first, and then Romans. Blacks were being oppressed. Even today, the oppressed, the poor, the imprisoned, the victims of racial and social discrimination, and the brokenhearted are still overwhelmingly Black. The West has sold the lie to Christians all over the world that Jesus was White. Historically, anthropologically, culturally, geographically, and biblically, we know that this is not true. Let the truth be known that the first human being (Adam) was created by God in his image, which was Black. Adam was created in Ethiopia, in Africa. When God decided to reestablish the liaison with mankind, he chose another Black man.

· If Blacks did not exist, there would have been no reconciliation with God because Jesus, a Black man, would not have been born.

· If Blacks did not exist, there would have been no Christian or Jewish religion, because the original Christians and Jews were Black.

AFRICA, BIRTHPLACE OF CHRISTIANITY

Africa is the cradle of Christianity and without Black people, Christianity would never have been born because White people (Romans) tried to prevent the religion from spreading. The contributors of the African Heritage Study Bible State:

> "The biggest distortion is the assumption that the Black Church began in the eighteenth century A.D. while omitting the fact that Ethiopia is the oldest Christian country in the world! Until recently, Blacks knew very little about Africa's contributions to the development of Judaism and Christianity during the formation of the early Christian Church. Among these are the fact: that there were many black saints, monastery life and work were developed in North Africa; African missionaries were sent into pagan Europe and at least three Western Popes were known to have been Black."[39]

For those who have some knowledge of the Bible, you may agree that there are missing pieces. There is an enormous gulf between the Old and New Testaments. Europe is not mentioned anywhere in the Old Testament. However, in the Old Testament, Africa is mentioned several times, Ethiopia is mentioned 40 times; and Egypt, more than 100 times. Africa and the Middle East were the main geographic locations in the Bible. In fact, Africa was connected to the Middle East when the Biblical events occurred.

Suddenly in the New Testament, Africa disappears from the Bible. Everything becomes White or Semitic. Everything is moved to Europe and the Middle East. Why? How can we explain this sudden transfer of geographic location? Rest assured, the truth will never be totally hidden.

The Acts of the Apostles describes the lives of the first Christians. It should normally tell the truth about their cultural origins. Most of this book was written by Luke, the physician, who followed Paul during his preaching missions. This book is a narrative masterpiece describing the time from Jesus' ascension to Paul's stay in Rome. Unfortunately, chronology is practically nonexistent. The language and thinking are Semitic (read Acts 1 to 12). Very often, the term "Jewish" is used to refer to Jerusalem or the cities or people around Jerusalem. Although the terms "Africa" and "African" were not mentioned, we can see through the marvelous stories, writing style, and epic characters that the New Testament was all about the activities of Blacks. The sources used by the writer of Acts are a mixture of orally told stories and written documents.

In Matthew 27:32 and Mark 15:21, it is written, "And as they came out, they found a man of Cyrene [an African village, in Carthage], Simon by name; they compelled to bear his (Jesus) cross." Simon of Cyrene, the man called to bear Jesus' cross while the soldiers were taking him to Golgotha to crucify him, was a Carthagian-African. Simon was visiting Jerusalem. He came from Cyranaic, North of present day Libya. Carthage was inhabited by Black people at that time. Simon of Cyrene became after Jesus' death, one of the first Christians in the history of the church.

Converting to Christianity was a big risk, an act of courage and bravery. It was almost suicidal to become a Christian. But they did it anyway and they were mostly Black. They had to hide, live together, and get baptized in the name of the Father, the Son, and the Holy Spirit in secret. Baptism was a way for them to prove their commitment to Christianity and their willingness to resist the oppressor. They had to put everything together and share what they had (Acts 2: 42-47). Many passages in the Bible, if read carefully, show that many Christians and prophets were Blacks at the beginning. Read, for example, Acts 13:1-3: "Now there were in the church that was at Antioch certain prophets and teachers; as Barnabas, and Simon that was called Niger, and Lucius of Cyrene, and Manan, which had been brought up with Herod the tetrarch, and Saul. As they ministered to the Lord, . . ." In this passage, Lucidius is from Cyrene. Cyrene is in Carthage and Carthage is in Africa. Northern Africa was inhabited by Black people at that time (Arabs occupied North Africa after 639 A.D.). Thus, Lucidius was Black. Simon was called *Niger*. "Niger" means "Black" in Latin. Also, *Manan* is a typical African name which can be found in the Akan ethnic groups in West Africa.

Christianity might have been completely vanquished were it not for the perspicacity of Abraha, Emperor of Ethiopia. Abraha converted himself to Christianity and decreed that this religion was the religion of his kingdom. He went to war against the persecutors of the Christians. He imposed that religion on the people and territories he conquered (Yemen, through Arabia and Mecca).

Many priests and bishops went to hide in Ethiopia as Christians were being massacred in Rome. If it were not for this Ethiopian emperor and other Africans, Christianity never would have grown.

Around the year 180 A.D., Christianity was firmly established in North Africa and all the territories of the former Egyptian empire. In 189 A.D., the first known Black African pope was elected. His name was Victor. He served his papacy in Rome, despite the massacre. He served as pope for 10 years. Pope Victor established a Church policy that is followed even today. He was the pope who decided that Easter should be celebrated on the Sunday following the fourteenth day of the vernal equinox. Pope Victor was not killed by the Roman emperor who also happened to be, by simple coincidence, a Black African Septimus Severus.

The second Black African pope was Melchiades, sometimes called Miltiades. He was elected in 309 A.D. Under his papacy, the Roman emperor decreed that it was no longer a crime to be a Christian. He allowed his citizens, the freedom to become Christians. Miltiades was the first pope admitted by Emperor Constantine to officially have his headquarters in Rome. He was the pope who chaired the first synod that was officially convened with imperial approval. Among the many policies he made, the most important one was the offering brought to the altar table so that the priest, bishop, or pope could bless it during the celebration.

The third Black pope was Gelasius (493-502 A.D.). He wrote a letter to Emperor Anastasius of Rome to tell him that there were two kinds of sovereignty on earth, the one that kings control and the one that God controls through the clergy. He made it clear to the emperor that no clergyman should obey any earthly king. Clergymen must only obey God. He wrote this letter following a conflict in which the emperor asked priests to obey his commands. Gelasius was the pope who established the separation between the church and the government.[40]

Africa was deliberately removed from the Bible in order to make Christians believe that Africa was not a historic part of Christianity. The truth is that the people in the Old Testament were of African descent and that Africa is the birthplace of Christianity. If Blacks did not exist, Christianity, the main religion in the Western world today, would not have existed, and Caucasians would still be adoring a throng of gods like the ones worshipped in ancient Greece and Rome.

THE ORIGINAL JEWS WERE BLACK

Today, many people argue that Jesus was not Black but Jewish. This, however, is a mistake because there is no such thing as a Jewish race. There is instead a Jewish culture. This section will therefore show that the original Jews (including Abram and Moses) were Black and came from Africa, and that Black people are everyone's ancestors by essence.

The original land of Jews where Abram lived was a Black land: Chaldee, south of Euphrates (Genesis 11:29-32). J. A. Rogers wrote that "Abram himself, must have been of the black race."[41] This thesis was already asserted by Godfrey Higgins who affirmed in 1927, "Chaldeans were Negroes."[42] Also, in his book, *From Babylon to Timbuktu,*[43] R. Windson says that Terah, Abram's father, came from Ur of the Chaldees. This can also be checked in the Bible (Genesis 11:27-32). Chaldeans belonged to the Cushite tribe. Cush was Ham's son and Ham was Black (Genesis 10:6-8). The Cushite tribe extended from the upper Nile Valley to today's Sudan. The original land of Abraham was not far from Egypt. One will therefore understand why the 75-year-old Abram was able to immigrate, so easily, by feet, to Egypt with his wife Sarai, his nephew Lot, and all the possessions they had accumulated (Genesis 12:9-20).

The book of Exodus explains how Moses, who was the son of Hebrew slaves, was miraculously saved. Because the

Egyptian Pharaoh wanted to kill all the Hebrew's newborns, Moses' biological mother put him in a basket on the river to save him. The river ran the little baby upstream, until he was found by Pharaoh's daughter. Afterward, baby Moses grew up in the palace as Pharaoh's daughter's son. In other words, Pharaoh's grandson (Exodus 2:1-10). No one suspected his racial or cultural origin. Everyone (including the Pharaoh himself) thought he was a child of the royal family. That is why no one contested him as the legitimate successor of the Pharaoh. This proves that Moses did not have a different skin color from the Black Pharaohs. Later, because of his good work, bravery, fairness, and leadership abilities, he was designated as the successor of Ramses, the Egyptian Pharaoh. One day, Moses discovered that he was the son of Hebrew slaves. He gave up everything, joined the Hebrew slaves, and took them out of Egypt to the "promised land."

The Bible says that only 70 Jews entered Egypt originally with Jacob (Genesis 46:27). The Bible also says that from Jacob (who was Moses ancestor) to Moses, the Jews lived 430 years as slaves in Egypt (Exodus 12:40). We also know that only 600,000 Jews left Egypt with Moses (Exodus 12:37). When Moses left Egypt with his people, there was a total of 3,154,000 Jews in Egypt.[44] So, from Jacob to Moses, this population multiplied 45,057 times in 400 years. It means that this population multiplied 112 times every year. Clearly, the majority of Jews (2,554,000) stayed in Africa. Maybe they stayed because of family matters or because they were living in other parts of the Egyptian empire (maybe in Ethiopia which was a part of the Egyptian empire), or maybe, the ones who remained were not slaves. Among those who stayed were the ancestors of the Falashas, the Black Jews, who live in Ethiopia today. The Jews who left with Moses were Black, and the Jews who stayed in Africa were Black. All the Jews were descendants of Jacob who was Black and who moved to Egypt 430 years earlier. Why should some of the people living on the same land, from the same ancestor, for the same amount of years be Black and others be White?[45]

In the Mohammedian Koran, it is written: "And Moses drew forth his hand out of his bosom and behold it appeared white unto the spectators." The commentator of this text added that Moses hands could not be white before and become white again after the miracle. The spectators were surprised that Moses hand became white. Scripture shows that Moses hand had a different color before. Anyway, they could not be white before the miracle. Moses was not White as he was portrayed in the movie *The Ten Commandments.*

Today, Jews who are excellent business people, can be found almost in every country in the world. Ion Robertson wrote in *Sociology*, "Many people, for example, consider the Jews a race. In biological terms, this view is nonsense. Jews have always interbred to some extent with their host populations, and many Jewish people are blond and blue-eyed in Sweden, small and swarthy in Eastern Europe, Black in Ethiopia, or Mongoloid in China."[46]   M. Fishberg wrote, "When the Jews live on a Black land, they are Black; on the land of the Brown man, they are Brown; on the land of the White man, they are White."[47]   Another writer, F. Hertz said, "In China, Jews are hardly dissociable from Chinese; in Africa, they are Black. In their expansion and talent as traders, Jews can be found almost everywhere and they adapt themselves, quicker than any one else, to the peoples they live with. But the original Jews were fundamentally Black. They were Blacks by essence."[48]

The truth is that the original Jews were Black. If Blacks did not exist, White Jews would not have existed, and no one would have lead the Hebrews to Palestine, and Israel would never have been created.

WHY DID EUROPEANS GO BACK TO AFRICA?

In the context of colonization, some people hesitate to incriminate European religious missionaries. They say that European missionaries were not the accomplices of the European administration. If these people are right, why did the European missionaries wait until colonization to decide to evangelize Blacks? Why didn't they attempt to evangelize Blacks between the tenth and the sixteenth centuries when Africa was experiencing a period of exceptional economic expansion?

This period of prosperity in Africa could have been an extraordinary opportunity for European missionaries to establish Christianity in Africa. Unfortunately, they did not do so. Their excuse was that Africa was too wild and too dangerous to be penetrated. Strangely enough, this excuse disappeared when Europeans decided to trade human beings as slaves. Africa stopped being too wild and too dangerous when they needed African raw materials to supply their industries.

For nearly 400 years, European missionaries watched their European contemporaries empty Africa from its human asset. Strangely enough, the European Christian ministry decided to establish Christianity in Africa at the same time Europe started its industrial revolution and colonization. All the evidence point to the fact that European missionaries were the accomplices of the European administration in the context of colonialization. European missionaries did not enter Africa innocently. As Aimé Césaire said, "No one engages in colonization innocently, no one colonizes with impunity. A nation that colonizes, a civilization that justifies colonization is already a sick civilization. It is a civilization that is morally contaminated and which, irresistibly, from consequence to consequence, from denial to denial, is calling on its own Hitler, I mean its own chastisement. Colonization dehumanizes man, even the most civilized man."[49]

For a long time, Europeans denied that African people believe in a supreme God. They treated African religious concepts as fetishism. In the United States, during the hard periods of slavery, Christianity was forbidden to African people, as if Africans had no right to receive the divine light and God's blessing. Later, in the United States, after African people were finally accepted into that religion, White people taught them a Christianity that required them to stay poor all their lives. White Christians told Black people they should renounce material wealth here on earth and wait for their reward after they die. Meanwhile, White people could be as rich as they wanted. Were White preachers talking about the same religion and the same God? A religion, when it is not understood, can be deflected and emptied of it essence. It can enslave people. In the context of the European evangelization in Africa, we will agree with Karl Marx that the Christian religion was "the opiate" of African people. Africans were drugged through White people's religious teaching.

To understand the essence of Christianity, one only needs to read the Acts of the Apostles in the Bible. The first Christians were unified, they put their belongings together and divided them according to each one's needs. They prayed assiduously. These elements were the essential components of Christianity: solidarity and prayer. Jesus himself summed this into two essential things: love God and love your neighbor. That was Jesus' answer to the Pharisees when they asked him: "Which is the greatest commandment in the law?" The first commandment according to Jesus is: "You shall love the Lord the God with all your heart, and with all your soul, and with all your mind." The second commandment is: "You shall love your neighbor as yourself." On these two commandments hang all the laws and the prophets (Matthew 22:34-40).

Since the time Europeans appropriated Christianity, this religion seems to have been emptied of its essence. Instead of emphasizing the socio religious aspects of Christianity, such as solidarity and love for one's neighbor, European evangelists emphasized materialism and individualism. On one hand, there were European missionaries who were born and raised in a materialist, violent, and self-centered environment. On the other hand, there was the African subconscious that was already prepared to receive Christianity. The Blacks were already living the principles of communal cooperation and love as Jesus taught.

Some people think that preachers and pastors inherited Jesus' powers. Many people go to church, expecting the priest or the pastor to mystically solve all their problems. Some clergymen aggravate the situation by not telling the truth. They entertain this myth.

European missionaries should have listened to the warnings given to them before they left their countries. In 1847, François Libermann wrote as a warning to the first missionaries sent to Africa:

> "The success of the mission relies upon you. At this time, your sins will be original. Do not judge at the first look. Do not judge according to what you have seen in Europe. Get rid of Europe, its mores, and its spirit. Make yourselves Negroes. Be their servants and serve them like a servant serves his master."[50]

In a penetrating study of the European colonization and missionary work, L. V. Thomas and René Luneau say that Christianity in Africa appeared indissociable from the presence of European militaries and merchants. This was its original sin. The history of the mission is, in a large part, one of the colonial conquest and the search for outlet and raw materials to supply European industries.

They elaborate further:

> "On one hand, there was an African society ruined and without any material means, slandered by three and half centuries of slave trade. On the other hand, there was a Western world, confident in its power and its rights, entering without complex, into its mission as a universal civilizer."[51]

For the missionaries, Africa was virgin territory, not a continent rich in history. For Europeans, Blacks were primitive people, curiously left out of the world evolution contest. Thus it did not matter that the African universe had been completely shattered.

Missionaries were not always obedient servants of the colonial administration, attests Louis Vincent Thomas. Nevertheless, for Africans, they were hardly dissociable from the civil servants working for the administration: same skin color, same language, same habits, and the same power. Luneau and Thomas wrote:

> "This power and the way the White man acquired it was at the origin of a redoubtable equivocalness that has not yet been dissipated in Africans' minds. The effects of this power continue to compromise very badly the future of African Christian communities."[52]

Defeated and colonized, Africans misinterpreted the source of the White man's power. They thought God himself supplied the power. Africans were outgunned, and did not stand a chance against their firepower. For Africans, however, every power is supplied from one's God. The ancestors, magician, and chief, each draws power from his God's energy. The techniques used to get this power are predefined and preset. How did the White man escape from these universal rules? How did the White man escape from the power of their protecting gods? Without searching further, Africans concluded that the success of the White man's weapon, his military strategy, and his technical prowess were transmitted to him by his God. Africans thought that the White man's

God gave him an extraordinary power against which the wisdom of their ancestors was powerless.

In the Bible, God fought alongside his people. His victories gave strength to the whole nation. Moses opened the sea to let his people go with the help of his God. Jesus Christ fed thousands of people by multiplying a few pieces of bread. The same Jesus resuscitated people who were dead for many days. He was able to calm down bad spirits and control the storms. Blacks started putting this religious teaching together with the reasons they were defeated. The conclusion was simple: the White man won the fight because his God fought for him. Blacks told themselves, "The God of the White man is a powerful one." Therefore, why would they not try to get the secret which the White missionaries were so generously offering them? If someone had told the Blacks that they did not lose the war because of the White people's God, they would not have believed him.

The power revealed by the White man during the war fascinated the African populations. Blacks, therefore, wanted to tap into the source of that power. The only way to do so, they were convinced, was to become Christians. This explains why, in the Protestant congregations, people read the Bible presented by missionaries as the source and the best way to understand the wisdom of God. Many African Protestants and all other religions derived from Protestantism (even today), page by page, scrutinized the Bible with an unconfessed hope to find the hidden secret that is in it.

Thomas and Luneau note:

> "To these starting ambiguities, were added some weaknesses, and ignorance. Catechism classes were flourishing at the beginning of the twentieth century. Young and old Blacks were learning like European children, sometimes with a hazardous translation in the local language. The teaching was very structured about the nature of God, the creation of man and the universe, and the rewards and chastisement depending on one's good or bad behavior."[53]

White priests introduced new cosmology to the Blacks. They talked about angels, those supernatural beings that God created just below himself and above human beings. The saints provided lessons about respecting God's laws. They were also interlocutors for human beings before God. If we take a close look at the whole religious teaching, we can notice that African peasants already knew God, man, the spirits, the saints, the ancestors (good or bad), right and wrong, happiness and sadness, solidarity, and mutual assistance between neighbors. Nothing essential was missing. It seems that the missionaries entered a system of evangelization that happened to be a substitution of terms and words.

European missionaries made African Christians recite prayers that they did not know the meaning. They gave the impression that Latin was the native language of Christianity. Religious celebrations conducted in Latin fascinated the African adepts.

European missionaries brought a mixed message of hope and oppression, salvation through Jesus Christ and hell through colonialism. Did the missionaries tell Blacks what they were saved from? If they were really saved, why did Blacks have to endure three and one half centuries of slavery? The Blacks were taught to wait for death to receive their rewards from God.

Europeans did not go back to Africa to teach them the Gospel of the Lord. European exploration went to Africa to search for the best lands to exploit. By the end of the nineteenth century, the entire African continent had been conquered and divided into small pieces, shared between European powers. This was the beginning of a second wave of exploitation (the first was the slave trade). Africa now belonged to Europe, and Blacks belonged to Europeans. Europeans made a profit between 100 percent and 150 percent. Through land rape, they supplied their processing industries with African raw materials and free African labor. Europeans would not have succeeded in their industrial revolution without Blacks.

WHAT WOULD EUROPE AND THE UNITED STATES BE WITHOUT BLACKS?

This section will explain how the Western civilization, as it is today, would not have been possible without Black people. From the Greeks to the Romans, from European capitalism to the rise of the American economy, Blacks were present at all levels in building Western civilization. Roman civilization was mostly inspired by Greek civilization. These two civilizations had many similarities. Therefore, in this section, we will only analyze the Greek civilization since the Roman one was born out of it.

Many White scholars, in an attempt to belittle Black people and to prove that nothing good has been made by Black people in the history of the world, try by any means to demonstrate that the Egyptian civilization was not forged by Africans. Yet, they assert that the Greek civilization was forged solely through the genius of the Greeks. Among these Caucasian scholars is Mary Lefkowitz,[54] who believes that many races coexisted in ancient Egypt. On the other hand, the ancient Blacks had outside help in building their magnificent empire, Greeks civilization was the sole product of Greek genius. She wrote,

> "The Greek philosophy as it was developed in the fifth and fourth centuries B.C. is fundamentally a Greek invention. It could not have been devised without the ability of the Greek language to express impersonal abstractions."[55]

What Mary Lefkowitz does not address is the fact that in the fifth and fourth centuries B.C., there were many foreigners living in Greece. For example, only 10 percent of the population living in Athens were authentic Athenians, according to Michael Curtis. In his book *Great Political Theories,* he indicates:

"The city-state of Athens in the 5th and 4th century B.C., with its 1,000 square miles of territory, its 40,000 citizens and 400,000 mixed population, remains one of the pinnacles of human civilization."[56]

Given such a diversified population, it is hard to believe that Greek civilization was exclusively a Greek invention and that Greeks built their civilization without any external contributions. Mary Lefkowitz makes the same mistake she made when she assumed that because Herodotus was not Egyptian he could not speak the Egyptian language. Lefkowitz's mistake is to assume that people who are not Greek citizens could not have mastered the Greek language. Without being a native speaker or citizen of a country, one can master the language of that country. Immigrants do it all the time. Lefkowitz's argument that the complexity of the Greek language prohibited external influences is superficial, to say the least.

It is a fact, however, that around 700 B.C., Egyptians enforced an immigration law forbidding Greeks to venture beyond the frontier of lower Egypt. They made this law because they considered Greeks as pirates and dangerous to national security. It was only under the ruling of Amasis that this law was progressively eased and later abolished. After that, many Greeks served as mercenaries in the Egyptian imperial army.

In 548 B.C., Thales (620-546 B.C.), the great Greek mathematicians and physicist went to Egypt to further his education. He studied astronomy, measurements of geometric quantities, theology, land surveying, and engineering. A few years earlier, Plato (with other students of Socrates) went to study the wisdom of Egyptian mythology.

After the Greeks conquered Egypt, they changed the name for it was originally Kmt (Kemet). Also, Pythagoras (born in 580 B.C.) went to Egypt to study science and philosophy. There, he discovered the rules of geometric figures and the right angle. Later, he returned to Greece to teach physics and mathematics. These examples go on and on.

One thing is certain: most of the great intellectuals, philosophers, and scientists who gave the world the essential formulas in geometry, medicine, mathematics, physics, and philosophy drew upon Egyptian knowledge. Greeks learned from Egyptians, and Romans learned from Greeks and Egyptians.

According to Diop, Neugbauer, and other historians, ancient Africans discovered writing, metallurgy, and geometry, and many of the exact sciences. Egyptians also invented the 365 $\frac{1}{4}$ day calendar which inspired the one used in the Western civilization today. Africa is, incontestably, the origin of Western civilization.[57]

Around 500 B.C., the Persians attempted to conquer Egypt, the Egyptians defeated them. Thirty years later, Herodotus visited Egypt and other parts of Africa. He noticed the wonders of the Egyptian empire. During that period in Meroe, the iron metallurgic industry was developing. Egypt was a great nation of interest to the entire world. It was so great that other nations sought to conquer it. Simultaneously, interminable conflicts started to develop inside the empire. These internal conflicts made Egypt a weak and vulnerable empire.

In 341 B.C., Persians attacked Egypt again. Finally, in 332 B.C., the army of Alexander the Great conquered Egypt. Alexander the Great founded the city of Alexandria as the capital of the new Greek empire. Alexandria became the biggest research center in the world. There the Greeks built the first library in history. The library contained some of Egypt's finest books and secret documents that were confiscated during the conquest.

Later, in 84 B.C., Rome conquered the Greece and became the leading world power. In 47 B.C., Emperor Caesar visited Egypt. Irritated by the truths he discovered in the Egyptian's books and documents, he confiscated them. He burned the library at Alexandria. In 30 B.C., Emperor Augustus of Rome annexed all of Egypt to the Roman empire. Europeans were long fascinated by Egypt's magnificence. During Egypt's peak, the rest of the world came to learn Egyptian philosophy, science, art, and technology.

From the decline of Egypt to the slave trade, Africa has been negatively affected with contact from the White world. Africa became the center of interest of Europeans whose imperialism was expanding toward America, which needed a labor force. At first, they tried to use indentured servants from Europe and the indigenous peoples, but were unsuccessful. They struck human gold when they "discovered" Blacks who produced the wealth for the European and American economies.

The enslaved Blacks worked, sometimes in groups of 100 or more and under a single master, on the cotton, indigo, sugar cane, and tobacco plantations. It was because of the Black labor force that White American farmers could save enough money to purchase machines during the industrial revolution. Black people's contribution was so important to the American economy that before 1620, agriculture in the country was very primitive. Blacks became its propelling engine, its unique machine. The result was incontestable. During the Civil War, the economy of the southern states was more prosperous than the economy of the northern states. This was because there were more Blacks working in the South than there were Blacks working in the North. President Lincoln's objectives were to preserve the Union and to fuel the northern economy which needed cheap labor for the industrial revolution. His objective was not to free the enslaved Blacks. He seriously pondered saving the Union by sending Blacks back home. The North objected for economic reasons. Europe and America were developing processing industries that needed raw materials unavailable in their respective areas. Again, Africa became the center of interests. Ki Zerbo wrote, "Africa, a worn out and exhausted continent, will successively become the object of scientific sympathy, the land of covetous interests, and the land of voracious appetite of the predator."[58] The turning point took place with the Berlin Conference in 1884. The major European countries literally divided Africa like a piece of pie. It took almost a century for African countries to secure their independence. They still suffer today due to neocolonialism. Many African leaders were trained in European schools and possess the values of their oppressors.

Today, the United States and Europe often intervene (under cover of the United Nations) in African, South American, and Caribbean conflicts. This was the case in Somalia in 1993, and in Haiti in 1994. These interventions seem to shock the Western public. Many Europeans and White Americans think that Black people should handle their internal affairs without the intervention of westerners. This raises strong debates inside some Western parliaments.

Westerners may be right to believe that Black people should handle their own affairs. However, they must not forget that Europeans destabilized Africa. Civil wars occur in Black countries because Europeans arbitrarily divided African ethnic groups into nation states designed to serve colonialism. The effect was to throw often warring groups together behind imposed borders, making them their will. Also, African wars are often instigated by European superpowers; a divided Africa is easier to rule.

Finally, Black people have served in Western wars that were so bloody, the White race could have been exterminated. During World War I, (1914-1918), 520,000 Black soldiers fought in the ranks of European armies. During World War II, 300,000 Blacks fought in the ranks of the allies. More than 165,000 Blacks lost their lives in that war that had little to do with them. At the Armistice in 1945, only 45,000 Black soldiers returned home.

On June 18, 1940, General De Gaulle (of the French army) made a desperate call to Blacks and other French soldiers and engineers who specialized in the weapons industry to help the cause of France. More than 70 percent of the French territory was occupied by Hitler. France and the allies were losing the war. French people had lost hope and thought it was impossible for France and the allies to win. Surprisingly, on a British radio station, General De Gaulle, who was exiled in London, declared, "Impossible is not French. France is not alone."[59] Given that the strategy of De Gaulle was to solicit the help of African people who had little military training, we can assume that what he actually meant was, "Impossible is not African."

He called on Blacks in the French colonies and entered France from the South. They pushed the German army from the South while Americans (among whom were also many Black soldiers) and Soviets attacked from the West and the East.

Anyway, "Europe got out of this war (the second World War), materially and humanly, prostrated. One million people were killed in France and in Great Britain. The National debt of France was 1,756 billion francs. Its infrastructure was demolished. Its battle fleet was annihilated. There was a moral laceration between collaborators and resistants which has left gaping wounds."[60] Europe owes a lot to Africa and Black people.

AFRICAN AMERICANS' CONTRIBUTIONS TO THE PROGRESS OF THE MODERN WORLD.

The great country of the United States of America was founded on the blood, death, and destruction of the Native Americans. It progressed on the blood, strength, and tears of the Black man. During the last few decades, there has been a movement in the Black communities to bring a more Africentric perspective into mainstream education so that all Americans could learn more about the contributions of Americans of African descent. Carter G. Woodson, a well-educated African American, started Negro History Week in 1926, to highlight the accomplishments of African Americans. Later, in 1976, it was realized that one week was not enough to cover so much information, and Negro History Week evolved into Black History Month. Today, we know that one month out of the year is not enough, and that the contributions of Black people to the history of the world should be presented all year long, right alongside those of other Americans.

Today, a rich and glorious legacy is starting to unfold. Never before have there been so many books and articles on African Americans that explain their historical significance in a positive manner. With this previously little known information comes a sense of pride, welcome relief to Blacks and African Americans who have endured hundreds of years of slavery and racism.

Benjamin Banneker, Frederick Douglass, Jan Matzeliger, Elijah McCoy, and many others tell a much different story from the old plantation scenario. Not only has this done wonders for the Black community, but it is beginning to paint a different picture for the rest of the society as well. Some of the things that were believed to have been invented by people of European descent seemed to carry a very strong African flavor. In *They Came Before Columbus*, Dr. Ivan Van Sertima tells of many African voyages to the Americas long before the birth of Christopher Columbus. It recounts the story of the Black man who piloted Columbus' ship and showed him the way to America.

Today, we know about the Black scientist, George Washington Carver, who discovered more than 300 uses for the peanut. Matthew Henson, a Black explorer, actually arrived at the North Pole before Admiral Perry and became the first human being ever to reach that point; however, most Eurocentric books say that Perry arrived first. Garret T. Morgan was an African American who invented the traffic light in 1923. He first gained fame when he invented the gas inhalators which saved construction workers trapped in a smoke-filled tunnel beneath Lake Erie. Fire department officials nationwide soon placed orders to buy the device. But many of them cancelled their order once they learned that Morgan was Black.[61] The ten cent coin bears the image of Franklin D. Roosevelt. This image was taken from the work of the African American artist, Selma Burke. Burke was born in Mooresville, N.C., in 1900. In 1935, she earned a Rosenwald Foundation Fellowship. She also won the Boehler Foundation Fellowship that allowed her to study in Europe for six years. During her stay in Germany, and at great risk to her personal safety, she smuggled food to German Jews who were in hiding from the Nazis.[62]

Most of us enjoyed the martial arts maneuvers of Bruce Lee back in the 1970s. Today, we see Chuck Norris, Steven Segal, Jean-Claude Vann Damme, and many others making a lot of money displaying their martial arts prowess. What many people do not know yet is that martial arts did not originate in Asia but in Africa. The editors of Ebony Man state:

> "Martial Arts is a spiritual learned science incorporating elements of African dances, music, mathematics, art, herbology, language, and other components, and its grace, cultural and artistic value aside, it remains a dangerous, formidable and practical form of self-defense."[63]

The following is a partial list of African American inventors and inventions (Compiled by "The Great Blacks in Wax Museum")

INVENTORS	INVENTIONS	YEAR	PATENT NO.
Allen, J.B.	Clothes Line Support	1895	551,105
Bell, L.	Locomotive Smock Stack	1871	115,153
Blackburn, A.B.	Railway Signal	1888	376,362
Boone, Sarah	Ironing Board	1892	473,653
Burr, J.A.	Lawnmower	1899	624,749
Carter, V.C.	Umbrella Stand	1885	323,397
Cooper, J.	Elevator Device	1895	536,605
Cralle, A.L.	Ice Cream Mold	1897	576,395
Davis, W.D.	Riding Saddles	1896	568,939
Downing, F.B.	Electric Switch for Railroad	1890	430,118
Ferrell, F.J.	Apparatus for Melting Snow	1890	428,670
Goode, Sarah E.	Folding Cabinet Bed	1858	322,177
Grant, W.B.	Golf Tee	1899	638,920
Hearness, R.	Detachable Car Fender	1898	628,003
Johnson, J.R.	Bicycle Frame	1899	634,823
Johnson, W.	Egg Beater	1884	292,821
Jones & Long	Caps for Bottles	1898	610,715
Latiner & Hichols	Electric Lamp	1881	247,097
Love, J.L.	Pencil Sharpener	1897	594,114

McCoy, E.J.	Lubricator	1882	255,433
McCres, D.	Portable Fire Escape	1890	440,322
Miles, A.	Elevator	1887	371,207
Purdy & Fatera	Design for Spoons	1895	24,288
Purdy & Sadgar	Folding Chair	1889	405,117
Purvis, W.B.	Fountain Pen	1890	419,065
Richey, C.T.	Railroad Switch	1897	587,657
Ricks, J.	Horseshoe	1886	338,781
Rillieux, N.	Sugar Refiner	1846	4,879
Scottron, S.R.	Curtain Rod	1892	481,720
Smith, J.W.	Lawn Sprinkler	1897	581,785
Spikes, B.D.	Automatic Gear Shift	1932	1,889,814
Stabdard, J.	Refrigerator	1891	455,891
Stewart, T.W.	Mop	1893	499,402
Washington, W.	Corn Musking Machine	1883	283,173
Woods, G.T.	Telephone System & Apparatus	1887	371,173
	Apparatus for Transmission		
	of Messages by Electricity	1895	315,368
	Electric Railway	1901	667,110
Wormley, J.	Life Saving Apparatus	1881	242,091

∧∧*∧*∧*∧*

African Americans have provided the world with illustrious figures in science, economics, politics, and culture. Today, in the streets of Paris, Munich, Brussels, London, and even Tokyo and Moscow, in almost every big city of the world, young people, dressed in baggy blue jeans worn down low in "Kris Kross" style and listen to rap music. That is today's fashion for young people. It is also the sign of the African American influence on the modern world. But more importantly, a Black American's influence is shown in the industries of sport, music and today, at a smaller lever, in the movie and television industries. An influence on music and sports is so serious that many White people and other racial groups mistakenly believe that sports and music are in Black people's blood, and that this is a gift from God, transmitted genetically from generation to generation. It seems today that if Blacks did not exist, sports, and the entertainment industries would be very precarious.

In athletics, during the 1936 Olympics, at a time when Adolf Hitler, the German fuehrer of the Third Reich, was fantasizing of world domination and extermination of Jews and Blacks, a young Black man, Jesse Owens, proved to the entire world that Blacks can be the best in anything if they put their minds to it and if they work toward achieving what they want. He won four gold medals during that Olympics. Black athletes have since dominated world athletics. Carl Lewis, Michael Johnson, Allen Johnson, Gwen Torrence, Jackie Joyner-Kersee, and Gail Devers are only few among the many Black athletes who have made this sport as exciting as possible. Blacks have transcended in other disciplines of sport with Dominique Dawes in women gymnastic, Evander Holyfield in boxing, Tiger Woods in golf, and Venus Williams in tennis.

The most prevalent field in which African Americans seem to have colonized the entire world is the field of music. For a long time, the entire world has been dancing under the rhythm of Black American music. Even rock and roll which, for a long time, was believed to be a White creation, is now known as a Black invention.

Author Kevin Chappell expounds:

> "It continues to be the biggest lie in the music industry -- that Whites created rock 'n' roll. From history books to rock-oriented cafes, from the pretentious Graceland mansion to the corner record store, White rock 'n' roll artists have been immortalized and credited with creating the multibillion-dollar rock music industry. Lost is the reality that rock 'n' roll was actually born out of the belly of Black blues music and raised by Black artists in the 1950s."[64]

Rock and roll music was born in the 1950s in smoke-filled clubs along Beale Street in Memphis, 47th Street in Chicago and 125th Street in Harlem. It was much later, after White teenagers had started digging the electric guitars and the pounding drum beats that African American artists were playing, that a White disk jockey (Alan Freed) changed the name of that music and re-named it "rock and roll." It was only then that White artists entered the capitalistic field of rock and roll.

White people disparagingly labeled the sound of rock and roll as "race" and "rhythm and blues" music. White artists entered the well-paying domain of rock and roll without shame. However, they didn't revolutionize the music. Lacking creativity, many White artists "covered" songs Blacks had written years earlier and made it big by copying the performing styles, dances and dress of Black artists like Little Richard, who even today can't believe how he and other Black artists were ripped off.[65]

Elvis Presley copied his song "Hound Dog" from Big Mama Thornton; Bill Haley copied his song "Shake, Rattle and Roll" from Big Joe Turner; and the Beatles copied their song "Roll Over Beethoven" from Chuck Berry. So did many other rock and roll artists who copied from Black musicians.[66]

Yes, Black artists invented rock and roll music. This is so true that Tim Moore, communication director for the Rock and Roll Hall of Fame and Museum in Cleveland confided to the reporter of *EBONY* magazine that, "It's sad but true. . . The music of the Black church and the music of the blues are the bedrock of what became known as rock and roll in the early 1950s."[67]

There is no need for us to mention here that Blacks are the inventors of jazz music with Duke Ellington, Louis Armstrong, and Miles Davis. Today, the jazz tradition is perpetrated by such artists as Wynton Marsalis, Grover Washington and Najee, to name only a few.

In the music industry, it is incontestable that Blacks have colonized the entire world. African American artists like Michael Jackson and Whitney Houston have transcended over all other musicians in the world and have dominated the pop and soft rock music. Since the early 1980s, 10 major recording artists have sold more than 325 million CDs, cassettes, albums and single records in the U.S., according to figures obtained from Recording Industry Association of America (RIAA). Almost half of the records sold were released by three artists -- Michael Jackson (62 million records sold), Whitney Houston (51 million records sold), and Mariah Carey (39.5 million records sold)."[68]

Also, in the 1980s, in order to denounce social discriminations, to express their frustration and to say what they could not say any other way, young African American groups and musicians such as Public Enemy, MC Hammer, Ice-T, Ice Cube, Sister Souljah and Queen Latifah, invented another line of music called *rap music* which has reached international prominence.

Black musicians "have changed the way we sing, dance and dream, moving America from be-bop to doo-wop to the modern age of soul, rock, pop, Gospel and beyond."[69] The talk show industry has been revolutionized by Oprah Winfrey who has been the leader for an unprecedented decade. Bill Cosby has had a similar affect on sitcoms, while Denzel Washington performs his charm on the silver screen.

PART TWO

PROPOSALS FOR

A NEW DEPARTURE

"We have allowed our adversaries to define who we are. And in politics as in life, when you allow your opponent to set the ground rules, it's hard to win."[70]

RAISING AWARENESS

According to a Zulu proverb from South Africa, "A person who kicks his own dog should not complain, nor be surprised, if someone else kicks him too." This proverb has a great social lesson: if Black people want respect from others, they must first respect themselves.

It is laudable that the Black community wants to cooperate with other cultural groups to build the society in which they belong. It is also admirable that Blacks want to prove they constitute a strong political and economic force. Sadly, however, the Black community fails to understand that if we want respect from others, we must first respect ourselves.

Unfortunately, too many African American youth think success can be obtained by any means necessary, including illegal ones. Our challenge is to create decent avenues toward material wealth, and more importantly, to measure wealth in the context of one's usefulness to the community and one's efforts toward assisting others. The European philosophy, "Every person fends for themselves," is so widely accepted that we no longer pay attention to community needs. A community cannot function without any social values. We need to rid ourselves of our common difficulties: poverty, crime against ourselves, drugs, juvenile delinquency, and unemployment. It is high time we understood that unity brings strength, and we have to look out for each other. The Black community has to be rebuilt at all levels, beginning with a foundation of solidarity.

Africans living in Western countries often renounce their cultural origins by claiming they do not know African traditions and customs. They do this because they think there is nothing valuable in Africa. How can others respect African values if we renounce them ourselves?

Problems exist between Caribbeans and Africans. Africans think that Caribbeans reject their African heritage. They think Caribbeans are reticent to team up with Blacks when it comes to business. They also think that Caribbeans are too westernized. On the other side, Caribbeans see themselves as unique and think that there is no point in looking to Africa to identify with their cultural heritage. We must go beyond these stereotypical considerations and together value the Black community and its cultural heritage.

To their credit, many other cultural groups show incredible unity and support within their communities. The reverse is true in the Black community. We prey upon one another and let others guide us or even buy our human dignity. If we do not heed this problem and we do not learn to solidify our community with respect and faith, we can not blame others if they do not treat us with respect, because "charity begins at home."

Caucasians have often been held responsible for Black people's pain and suffering, whether it is in Africa, South America, the United States, or the Caribbean Islands. This is true on many fronts, especially if we look at things from a historical point of view. Of course, Black people have paid very hard for their historical contacts with Europeans. But, should these historic experiences excuse our sense of hopelessness and apathy? Should this make Black people give up the fight?

It is time for Black people to get organized and stop complaining. Let's stop begging others and begin to rely on ourselves. Our happiness depends on ourselves; it depends on an internal organization between ourselves and on strong solidarity among our peoples.

It is time for Black people to stop killing each other and become a homogenous group and fight hand in hand against racial, political, and economic discriminations. It is time Black people around the world clear their minds of the false and mendacious ideas that portray Blacks as lazy, incapable of creating anything on their own, good for nothing, or uncivilized. Every thing Black is not inferior and bad. Should Black people learn everything from the West? It is time for Blacks to learn their history from an Africentric perspective. It all depends on us. If we do not become aware that we must organize, if we do not realize that unity is strength and that we must join our efforts in order to gain back our cultural identity and our political and economic freedom, then there should be no one other than ourselves to blame.

Women's role in society has been the object of many writings in the past couple decades. It has also been the subject of many debates and polemics. In Africa, men are blamed and accused of treating women like second class citizens, slaves, or sex objects. In the United States and in Europe, one has often argued that "equality" between men and women is only a wretched theory; the ditch between men's and women's responsibilities is wide and deep. Trying to hide these sexual prejudices, politicians in almost every country, especially during election campaigns make statements that are only politically correct, not truthfully correct.

Despite women's many cries for help, their situation does not seem to have improved much; that is because men (who do not seem to have abandoned their traditional ideas regarding women) have not yet understood the potential contribution of women in the economic process. They have not understood that our society will improve when more women become involved in economics and politics.

In an excellent study entitled, *Women in Economic Development,* the department of Africa at the World Bank enumerated many serious sexual discriminations in Africa. According to this study, sexual discriminations in our modern societies are so severe that they negatively impact upon the development process. Most of these discriminations are circumscribed in the access to productive economic resource, transport, wage earning, and the law. Through my research, I discovered that most of these discriminations can be observed in Western countries as well.[71]

Cases studied by the World Bank show that in Africa, the gender imbalance between men and women in access to economically productive activities leads to a lower response to economic potential. Even in industrialized countries, some activities are classified as exclusively reserved to women and some reserved to men. For example, in the United States, it is perceived as "diminishing" for a man to be a baby sitter because it's considered a woman's job. Other examples include being a secretary or a nurse. Also, in the United States, most of the time, when a husband finds a new job in a different state, the woman must quit her job because the whole family has to move with the man. Even when the woman's loss of revenue cannot be compensated by the husband's new income, she must still quit her job and move with her husband. The interest of the woman is hardly considered.

The reverse is rarely true, men rarely quit their jobs, follow their women, and baby-sit.

The World Bank experts observed that in Kenya for example, value of women's output would increase by 22 percent if they had the same access as men to resources and factors of production-maize weeding. The experts at the World Bank observed that in Ghana for example, men spend 346 hours a year on transport work, carrying 12.1 tone/km; women spend 977 hours a year, carrying 46.6 tone/km. Women spend 236 hours a year collecting water (men: 17 hours a year) and 82 hours a year collecting firewood (men: Eight hours a year). They also observed that in Burkina Faso, on Central Plateau, women spend 565 hours for water collection and in market 380 hours a year.

Gender discriminations exist in democratic and developed countries. In the United States, White women's median income is 80 percent of male income (Black income is 60 percent of White income) and if there is a divorce she experiences a major loss in her standard of living. Democratic America has never had a female president or vice-president, while electing 44 White males. Also, in almost every country, it is the woman who must abandon her family name when there is a legal marriage. The term maiden name only applies to women, never to men. In Mali, the marital code restricts a woman from opening a business without her husband's authorization. In South Africa, under customary law, women remain perpetual minors. In some African countries, women lose their children to the husband, if they opt to divorce.

In order for African people to reach their full potential – women must be fully empowered. Sexism in our society mirrors the behavior at home. Men must be reeducated to value women, while simultaneously women must demand respect. Rape and wife abuse can't be tolerated by a people committed to freedom. African women are needed in boardrooms, hospitals, classrooms, outer space, cyberspace, and at home nurturing the next generation. We need a culture that will empower women.

STRENGTHENING COOPERATION AMONG AFRICANS WORLDWIDE

For many Blacks living in the West, Africa is a country, not a continent divided into countries like Europe, America, or Asia. When one talks about Africa, westerners think of the aridness of its lands, hard sunshine, abundant vegetation, or desert. Many westerners' mental image of Africa is a continent inhabited by lazy people who die of endemic diseases. In westerners' mental image, Africa is inhabited by a population that is daily decimated by the hundreds, because of starvation and interminable civil wars. They also imagine an African continent filled with wild animals living alongside Black men and women who live in primitive conditions. When you speak about African politics with westerners, they think of dictatorial, barbarian, totalitarian, or monarchical governments. Africa is viewed as a continent that does not inspire human dignity; everything seems to go against what is called "civilization."

Like White people and other cultural groups, some African Americans and Caribbeans see Africa as a continent that has not performed evolution. Therefore, they refuse to visit or to learn about Africa. Many African Americans think of Africa based solely on Western media. They have the same mental predisposition as White people to believe that their motherland has nothing valuable to offer them. If an African, during a discussion or a debate, proves that he has certain intellectual baggage or that he is very knowledgeable, they look at him with astonishment because they believe that Africa is too poor to educate its people.

Wealthy African Americans refuse to invest in Africa. Some African diplomats in the United States told us the following: "When we contact them to invest in Africa, they respond that they will not take a risk to invest in a country where the government can be overturned anytime by militaries who will confiscate their businesses."

Other African American business people refuse to invest in Africa. They say, "Blacks are too involved with their traditions; they are technically retarded, and too poor." Other African Americans, such as author Keith Richburg mentioned earlier, think that they are fortunate because of slavery to live in America.

There is an obvious lack of information about Africa and African people. There is a media campaign designed to portray African people negatively. Many African Americans who visit Africa are amazed at the plush hotels and business centers after watching numerous famines the media loves to portray. Unfortunately, the majority of African Americans may never visit Africa to see the reality. It reminds me of the same U.S. media that covers our murders, but not our constructive programs. There is also a malicious intent aimed at dividing Black people.

Blacks must infuse the curriculum from primary schools to colleges with Africentricity in every subject. These programs must be objectively taught by Black teachers or people who have a clear knowledge of African, Caribbean, and African American people and their history and cultures. They must also elucidate the truths about Africans. Education and culture are the tools toward empowerment.

Africans must also have greater access to electronic media to achieve the same objective. This will create pride among Africans worldwide. This can also help us be proud of our mother continent. It is imperative that African youth, be proud of their heritage. Self-hatred breeds senseless violence in our neighborhoods. We must search for ways to unite. It is time we start looking at each other like people from the same race, not Blacks from different places. It is a good thing to call each other "brothers and sisters," but these should not be empty words. Real brothers and sisters do not kill each other. They help and look after each other.

In the United States, many African Americans wear African clothes, but do not visit Africa as opposed to other parts of the world. Does this mean that they do not care much about their motherland? What can be done? It has been argued that African Americans do not show much interest in Africa, their motherland.[72]

We must organize trips and excursions from America to Africa and the islands. During these excursions, each participant will be adopted by an African family. These African families will adopt them as brothers and sisters, sons and daughters (and vice versa). This will allow African Americans and other Blacks to feel physically and spiritually connected to a home where they can go any time in their motherland.

Many African leaders have hired Caucasians for technical assistance. These Caucasians secure significant contracts. Blacks from the Diaspora and African leaders must network. There are many African Americans technically qualified, but are unwilling to work in Africa, and others are willing but are unqualified. We must create African employment agencies in America. At all levels, we must strengthen the communication among Blacks worldwide.

My personal experience and many studies have proven that African Americans are very much interested in purchasing products that are related to their African cultural heritage. This means that the United States can be an important niche for African products. But, for this to be possible, Blacks must do more than they are doing today so that they can become more competitive economically on the American market for Africentrist products. African countries can reduce their external debt, increase their gross national product (GNP), improve their economic growth, and be very competitive in the global world economy if they export more products toward Western industrialized countries and import less from them. The best way to do so is for African governments to address certain macroeconomic conditions that inhibit the development of an export industry.

In an excellent study entitled, *Africa Can Compete*, Tyler Biggs, Gail R. Moody, Jan-Hendrick Van Leeuvan, and E. Diane White sustain that there is a significant demand in the United States for Africentric products such as standard African clothing. The authors support their conclusions by several case studies of the United States retailers and buyers and their interactions with African suppliers for three categories of products: Africentric clothing, Africentric home products, and conventional attire. The retailers included JCPenney, Montgomery Ward, Kmart, Dayton Hudson, and Pier 1 among retailers. They also interviewed middle distributors such as Associated Merchandising Corporation (AMC). On the supply side, they conducted their research in five countries (Ivory Coast, Ghana, Kenya, Senegal, and Zimbabwe) to evaluate the opportunities and obstacles for African suppliers entering the U.S. market.[73]

Africa's competitiveness in the manufacture of standardized garment, observe the authors, is that all but two African countries are quota free (Lesotho and Mauritius being the exceptions). This advantage is critical. The potential market is huge: a one percent increase in U.S. apparel imports would represent an increase of close to $275 million per year, more than 10 times the current apparel exports of the five countries considered in the study.

Some experts believe that most of the supply problems that emanate from the mismatch between U.S. buyers requiring large volumes and adherence to strict delivery schedules, quality specifications, and small manufacturers with little export experience and no familiarity with U.S. business culture.

They say that African suppliers are not yet sophisticated enough to meet the rigorous demands of foreign buyers, often producing products of inferior quality and experiencing problems in packaging and the coordination of input supply.

- Technical assistance is required for on-site training in producing methods, quality control, and technical craft skills. This includes teaching artisans how to manage production schedules, accurately judge material input requirements, and get goods to a pre-established collection point on time.

- Working capital must be made available so firms are able to meet large orders immediately and update their technology.

- Better management is necessary. African managers, long conditioned to domestic market which generally absorbs merchandise without respect to quality and price, must strengthen themselves to survive the rougher competition of the international marketplace.

- Better access to information is needed, especially concerning the complexities of the foreign retail systems, the positioning of retailers, and the retailers who offer the greatest promise as customers.

At the same time, the study indicated that African governments need to address certain macroeconomic conditions which inhibit the development of an export industry.

- The ability to import raw materials at world prices with the minimum of difficulty is essential for success in global trade. In too many African countries, red tape and bureaucratic restrictions still abound, raising the cost of doing business and deterring potential entrants.

- Governments also have a key role to play in eliminating anti-export bias in their exchange rate regimes. In all five countries studied, despite widely varied approaches to managing the exchange rates of their currencies, all companies surveyed reported difficulties in obtaining foreign exchange.

- Finally, unless addressed, infrastructural deficiencies could put a quick halt to further growth of exports. Port facilities and roads in the countries need to be studied. Telecommunications facilities, increasingly important in international business, also need to be strengthened.

WHAT CAN BE DONE IN THE UNITED STATES OF AMERICA?

As a teacher, I noticed that every time I asked my Black students to work in groups of two with a White or an Asian student on a specific assignment, these Black students felt very uncomfortable. They preferred working with a Black peer. Then, one day, one of them told me that he did not want to look dumb in front of a White or an Asian student. I asked him why. He responded that Asian students focus too much on their studies and that he didn't have the time to do the same. He said, "If I don't study as much as he does for this assignment, I will look dumb in front of the whole class." As for the White students, he believed that they are naturally successful. He said, "They know why they go to school. They know they will find a good job as soon as they graduate from school. So, they try hard. He also told me, "Look around, how many Black students become high professionals or millionaires after their studies?"

For Black youth, the challenge is to become proud of their African cultural heritage and to broaden their horizons. One way to help them do this is to present them with more professional Black role models from within their own communities. But is that not another challenge? Is it indeed possible to find Black role models in every professional field? Are Black youth exposed to an uncertain future because they look upon White people as role models and lack Black role models? We need every positive African American adult both blue-collar and white-collar to mentor our youth. *Our youth suffer from a deficit of adult-child interaction.*

Today, African American people are walking away from our values and norms. The younger generation is not utilizing the church as a resource and anchor. Historically, the church has been the backbone of the family since slavery. We need churches developing ministries attractive to youth and males. Too many churches only attract elders and women. Isn't it ironic that the group least represented – young Black males – is least represented in our best institution.

An African adage stipulates that the best way to prevent a thief from stealing, is to put him in charge of the thing you want to safeguard. Only a thief knows the prevention techniques against robbery. It is also a thief who knows the place other thieves hide themselves.

This adage can be applied to real life. A person who steals does not feel responsible for what he steals because what he steals does not belong to him. If this thief is not caught, he is not accountable to anybody, except to his own conscience. Since conscience is a relative term, it may apply to one person while others may not care at all. It all depends on the way we are raised. One thing is sure: a thief does not steal his own properties.

This adage can help reduce crime in the African American community. Most crimes in the Black communities can be avoided if Black youth become more responsible. We put them in charge, and make them feel responsible. We must help them to participate in the life of their communities.

Why do young Black people join gangs? Generally, young people join gangs to secure nurturance that was missing from home. Gangs give them shelter and psychological and material comfort. If we take a close look at gangsters' lives, we notice that they have a great sense of solidarity and cooperation. They look after each other and have a great sense of mutual assistance.

We know that most gangsters, even the cruelest ones, do not kill the members of their own gang. We also know that gangsters look after one another and assist each other. When a member of a gang is arrested by the police and sent to jail, the other members do not abandon him because he is in jail. When he gets out of jail, he is welcome. They explain to him the new gang rules and strategies. They support him materially and psychologically. Then they give him new responsibilities. He is accepted again by his gang. On the other hand, people of his community look at him like an ex-con, a dangerous person. They refuse to hire him in their businesses. They reject him. Why did we not welcome him back into society and turn him into an upstanding citizen? Let's create a committee that would reconcile our youth back to the community. We need to make our youth more responsible and useful in their neighborhoods.

In Abidjan, the Ivory Coast, in a city called Abobo, a group of young adult gangsters changed their way of living by turning their gang into a security guard business. This happened because of the advice of a retired police officer. The old man who had been living in the neighborhood for a long time knew most of these former gangsters personally and advised them to do something positive in their community instead of destroying it. Fortunately, they listened to him. Since then, in exchange of the neighbors' financial contributions, these young people watch the neighborhood day and night. The inhabitants of this neighborhood feel more secure today and crime has been drastically reduced in the neighborhood.

Two years after they started their business, they opened a small community center for young people who have disciplinary problems. When these former gangsters notice misbehavior from any young person in the neighborhood, they make him come to the center and integrate him in one of their programs. The program works very well because the founders understand the youth. Today, they work in collaboration with the local police. Another one told us, "Being in charge of the security of the community makes us feel more responsible. It is like taking care of your own relatives. It is no game at all because if you fail, the whole community is in danger."

To start with, we must organize ourselves and our communities. Black men and women must be concerned about what is going on in their communities. We must tell ourselves that these gangsters could be our own children, brothers, or sisters. We must talk to them and listen to their concerns. Talking to them does not mean insulting them or humiliating them. Talking to them means, firstly, to listen and understand them. Secondly, it means through a discussion, identify a solution suitable to everyone. It is important to make these young people understand that they have no reasons to join a gang because they can be more useful doing something positive in their communities. Of course, convincing the leaders of the gangs (who benefit from being gangsters) will be more difficult, but it is possible. These leaders must understand that they can turn their gang into a positive group in the community. It requires courage and organization. Our youth were not born dangerous. They become what they are today because of a combination of social circumstances. Many of them do not like what they do. They can change if we help them.

Black people must also understand that shooting each other will not solve conflicts or misunderstandings. We must agree to sit down and talk. Communication can help solve many problems between our people. We must learn to be afraid to die or to get hurt. Today, it seems that many Black youth are not afraid to die. If they are not afraid of losing their own lives, why would they be afraid to take the life of someone else?

It is important that we teach our young Black brothers and sisters the importance of life through a progressive education. Parents must help their children to value their lives, help them to develop goals. A person who has a goal in life is afraid to die. We must help our children understand that they can have a great future if they set goals and make plans. We must teach them to distinguish between right and wrong, between what is socially accepted and what is not. For example, they must understand that a hero is not a person who kills. Helping them value the human race can be a good starting point. We must take them to a place of worship. This will help them understand the value of solidarity, love, self-esteem, and respect of one's neighbor. Our Black youth must understand the value of working hard. By learning the value of hard work, they will learn to stay away from easy drug money, they will respect what belongs to their neighbors, and will think twice before taking what does not belong to them through robbery, violence, and killing. Black youth must grow up with the idea that if they try hard enough, they can get the most out of life.

In addition, Black youth must face the realities of life. They must be introduced to crime victims in hospitals. They must come to understand the pain and suffering that crime victims endure. Author Jawanza Kunjufu, recommends field trips to other places besides museums, zoos, planetariums, and art galleries. Our youth need to visit a jail or prison, criminal court, drug abuse programs, and emergency rooms at public hospitals.[74]

CONCLUSION

What if Blacks did not exist? had two goals: First, to reestablish long hidden and twisted truths about people of African descent. Second, to raise awareness and to propose unity among African people worldwide. In the first part, we explained that Africans contributed greatly to world development. Without Africans, many things would not have succeeded in the world and especially in Western civilization.

The important objective was to rectify some historical facts and encourage Black youth, that their ancestors were present everywhere, from the beginning.

African people must come together, hand in hand, for the same cause. We must unite as a big and strong family; we must help each other, and look after each other. Africans in America must collaborate with Africans from the continent, Caribbean, and wherever Africans reside.

In May 1963, on the initiative of the Guinean president, Sékou Touré; supported by Patrice Lumumba; President Kwame Nkrumah (Ghana); Hailé Selassié, Emperor of Ethiopia; and thirty-one African chiefs of states met in Addis Abeba (Ethiopia) and founded the Organization of African Unity" (O.A.U.). The objectives of the O.A.U. were to reinforce unity and cooperation among all African states (including Madagascar and other African islands), to built an united African army that would defend the frontiers of Africa, to protect African people against any European interference in African economic and political affairs, to protect human rights in Africa, and to have a unified economic management.

Unfortunately, these laudable projects were never exploited. The leadership of Nelson Mandela and the African National Congress have been encouraging. The work of Leon Sullivan and the African Summitt has been excellent. We must build on these movements. The success of The Million Man March and the Million Woman March were proof that African people can unite on a large scale.

The first objective is to convene an international meeting of African people. This organization should include African heads of states (O.A.U.), Caribbean heads of states, two representatives from each African and Caribbean state, two hundred African American representatives, four per state (one man, one woman, two youths: male and female). It would also include a male and female representative from other countries where Africans reside.

THE GOALS OF THE MEETING ARE:

- To revitalize our race.

- To prove to ourselves we can be unified.

- To allow African leaders to identify and solve problems.

- To encourage socialization and cultural exchange between African people worldwide.

- To facilitate exchange of information and life experiences among African people.

- To strengthen our economic conditions and reduce unemployment.

- To find strategies to facilitate cultural and technological exchange.

- To promote African cultural values and reestablish the truth about African history.

- To reduce crime.

- To create a worldwide media network.

THE ORGANIZATION COULD BE FINANCED
AS FOLLOWS:

- **Contributions of the participating countries:** If each member state contributes $10,000 per year (including each American state); this would generate $1 million annually.

- **Contributions of individuals:** If 2 percent of the 950 million Africans in the world contributed $1 per year, it would generate $19 billion.

- **Interest:** Monies could be deposited in an interest bearing account and generate another $40 million.

We believe African people worldwide should create a month of reconciliation and peace. This will be an occasion for our people to get together, talk, and solve our differences. In the spirit of the Million Man March, October can be our month of atonement. The month should emphasize praying and fasting.

- The first task is to create in every neighborhood, a committee that will register all conflicts between Africans. These committees will try to solve conflicts and disputes involving African people.

- The committees will also be in charge of bringing together African families in the neighborhood to collaborate.

- Before the month ends, conflicts should be resolved. A journal or a magazine created for the occasion should publish all the resolved conflicts.

- A feast should conclude the month which would include food, music, and dancing.

CREATING AN ECONOMIC FUND TO SUPPORT BLACK COMMUNITIES

Every year, millions of American workers (including African people) contribute to the presidential campaign fundraising. They do this when they are filing their tax return.

During a professional training in Washington, D.C., we found out that many Black people donate money to the education of our youth. These contributions constitute a significant amount of money that is managed by an association called "The Black Student Fund," located in northwest Washington, D.C. This fund helps many Black youth from low income families to attend good private schools in the metropolitan area.

Given our track record of giving, surely we could create a national Black fund to help our Black communities. We certainly have the resources.

- 14 percent (about 1,120,000 Blacks) of African American households have an annual income over $50,000.

- If each household with an income above $50,000 a year agrees to contribute $5 per month, we can reach the amount of $67,200,000 per year from this category only.

- If all the households earning between $25,000 and $50,000 per year agree to contribute $3 every month, we can reach the amount of $247,680,000 per year from this second category.

- Put together, the contributions of these two categories will make a total of $314,880,000 per year.

- If the many Black American millionaires agree to contribute, we can reach a total substantial amount that could be reinvested, year after year, into the creation of investment banks or credit unions for Black people who have good business projects. These banks could finance investment projects, businesses, educational projects, health care projects, scholarships, community security programs, and crime and drug prevention.

CREATING PARTNERSHIPS TO START
OUR OWN BUSINESS

We conducted a survey in Washington, D.C., and the states of Virginia and Maryland. We questioned 200 young Black Americans between the ages of 21 and 35 about their spending habits. The survey gave the following results:

- 35 percent of these youths spend about $24 every month to buy alcohol, 13 percent spend more than $30 a month buying cigarettes, and 19 percent spend about $11 a month to rent video tapes.

- 8 percent spend more than $100 a month on dates.

- 97 percent of these youths admit that they can reduce these expenses by more than half if they tried.

- Each of them spend at least $200 for things that are not really indispensable.

- 91 percent work for a White owned business.

- Almost all of them (98 percent) wish to have their own business, but do not know where to find start-up funding.

We asked them if they had ever thought about associating with other Blacks as partners to create their own businesses. They were hesitant. Their reasons are understandable:

- Who would manage the business?

- What are the guarantees in a partnership?

- What will happen if a partner wants to withdraw his shares from the partnership?

- What happens when we disagree?

- Would the business be competitive in this global economy?

In closing, African people built the first civilization. If our ancestors could build pyramids that remain standing, surely we can build institutions by pooling our resources together. We are not the minority unless we allow ourselves to be identified based on where we were deported by boat. In the spirit of an African, Marcus Garvey, born in Jamaica, who came to the United States, "Up you mighty race, you can accomplish what you will."

FOOTNOTES

Introduction

1. P. Gaxote, *La Revue de Paris,* Paris, October 1957, p.12.

2. Asa G. Hillard, in the introduction of the book, *Stolen Legacy*, by G. M. James, 1976, Marcus Books, San Francisco, p. 7.

3. Mary Lefkowitz, *Not Out Of Africa: How Afrocentrism Became An Excuse To Teach Myth As History,* A New Republic Book, New York, NY, 1996.

4. Herodotus, *Book II*, p. 100, translated by George Rawlinson, New York: Tudor, 1928.

5. Karl R. Lepsius, as quoted in *Civilization or Barbarism,* by Cheikh A. Diop, Lawrence Hill Books, Brooklyn, New York, 1991, p. 17.

6. Joseph Ki Zerbo, *History of Black Africa*, Paris, Hatier, 1978, p. 62.

7. Joseph Ki Zerbo, *History of Black Africa*, Paris, Hatier, 1978, p. 58.

8. Joseph Ki Zerbo, ibid., p. 63.

9. Tudor Parfitt, *Journey to the Vanished City*, Saint Martin Press, New York, 1987. The whole book, written by a White Britain, is about the lives of Black Jews in South Africa.

10. *The Original African Heritage Study Bible*, James C. Winston Publishing Company, 1993, pp. 82 - 83: *The last great dispersion, in A.D. 135*; Joseph Ki Zerbo, *History of Black Africa*, Hatier, 1978, Chronological index.

11. *The Dawn of European Civilization, The Dark Ages*, Edited by David Talbot Rice, McGrow-Hill Book Company, Inc., New York, London, 1965, pp. 53 - 54; and Cheikh Anta Diop, *Civilization or Barbarism: An Authentic Anthropology*, translated from the French by Yaa-Lengi Meema Ngemi, English version, Lawrence Hill Book, 1991, p. 23.

12. *The Original African Heritage Study Bible*, op. cit., p. 1813.

Chapter 1

13. Fernand Braudel, as quoted in the preface of the book, *History of Black Africa*, by Joseph Ki Zerbo, op. cit. p. 5.

14. *Holy Bible* (King James vesrion), in Genesis, 9:18-27.

15. Voltaire, in *Essai sur les Moeurs*, Volume I, p. 1829.

16. Montesquieu (1698 - 1775), *"Esprit de la Loi"*, Book XI, chapter V, p. 327.

17. Richard J. Herrnstein and Charles Murray, *The Bell Curve: Intelligence And Class Structure in American Life*, The Free Press, New York, NY, 1994.

18. Cheikh Anta Diop, *Civilization or Barbarism: An Authentic Anthropology,* translated from the French by Yaa-Lengi Meema Ngemi, Lawrence Hill Book, New York, 1991, p.11.

19. Joseph Ki Zerbo, *History of Black Africa*, Paris, Hatier, p. 51.

20. Joseph Ki Zebo, ibid., p. 51.

Chapter 2
21. Keith B. Richburg, *Out of America: A Black Man Confronts Africa,* Basics Books, Harper Collins Publishers, Inc., New York, NY, 1997.

22. Comment from William Finnegan, the commentator of "The Book Review," in the *New York Times*, Sunday, March 30, 1997.

23. Hegel, *Cours sur la Philosophie de l'Histoire,* Paris: Albin Michel, 1830, p. 505.

24. *History of Black Africa,* op. cit., p. 407.

25. As Blaise Pascal, a french philosopher said, what is true here may be wrong somewhere else: "What is true on one side of the Pyrenees, can be wrong on the other side," In *Pensées de Blaise Pascal,* Hachette, 1958, p. 48.

26. Yves Brillon, *Ethnocriminology of Black Africa*, P.U.M., Montreal-Paris, 1978, p. 28.

27. Felix T. Ehui, *Raising Awareness on the Situation of Women in the African Societies, The Bridge-Le Pont magazine,* June 1995, Volume II, No. 1, p. 18.

28. Felix T. Ehui, ibid.

29. The *Bambaras* are the biggest cultural group in West Africa. They can be found in modern Mali, Sierra Leone, Burkina-Faso, Niger, and in the Northern regions of Ivory Coast.

30. *Oral Literature*, Colloquium on Black Art, Présence Africaine,1967, pp. 243-248.

Chapter 3

31. Frossard, *La Cause des Esclaves Nègres,"* Vol. II, A. Delaroche, Lyon, 1789, p. 68.

32. Ibrahima Baba Kaké, *Au Temps des Grands Empires Africains*, Paris: Hachette, 1991, p. 12.

33. Senghor was the first President of Senegal. Today, he is the only Black member of the French Academy.

34. This is why today one finds Hutus in Burundi and Rwanda; Evhés in Ghana and Togo; Sénoufos in Burkina-Faso, Mali and Ivory Coast; Abrons in Ghana and Ivory Coast; and Yacouba in Ivory Coast and Liberia.

Chapter 4

35. Professor, Reverend Cain Hope Felder, Ph.D., *The Original African Heritage Study Bible*, James C. Winston Publishers, Inc., 1994, Introduction, XV.

36. *The Bridge-Le Pont magazine*, Volume II, No 3, November 1995.

37. Reverend Willie Wilson, the Union Temple Baptist Church, South East, Washington, D.C., in *The Bridge-Le Pont magazine*, Volume I, No. 3, November 1995.

38. The Bridge-Le Pont magazine, op. cit., p. 21.

Chapter 5

39. Professor Reverend Cain Hope Felder, Ph.D., *The Original African Heritage Study Bible,* James C. Winston Publishers, Inc., 1994, pp. 1813-1816.

40 *100 Amazing Facts About the Negro*, by J. A. Rogers, Helga M. Rogers, St. Petersburg, Florida, 1985, pp. 9-36, and *Blacks Before America,* by Mark Hyman, Africa World Press, 1993, pp. 103-106. For more information about the Black Popes, please, read *The Books of the Popes*, p. 17 for Pope Victor, p. 110 for Pope Miltiades, and p. 40 for Pope Gelasius. Read also *The white Africans*, Paris, 1910, p. 83.

Chapter 6

41. J. A. Rogers, *100 Amazing Facts About the Negro,* Helga M. Rogers' Publication, Florida, 1957, p. 57.

42. *Chaldeans were Negroes,* by Godfrey Higgins, Anapocalypsis, Volume II, p. 364, New York, 1927.

43. R. Windson, *From Babylon To Timbuktu,* New York, 1910, pp. 97-121.

44. *History of Ethiopia*, by L. J. Morie, Volume II, pp. 18-183, Paris, 1904.

45. Under the leadership of Queen Judith, the Falashas or Ethiopian Black Jews started Solomon's lineage. Later, under the leadership of Sheba, they overthrew the Ethiopian emperor in 938 A.D. and ruled the Ethiopian empire for 40 years. Emperor Haile Selassie was a Falasha Jew.

46. Ion Robertson, *Sociology*, 3rd edition, 1987, Worth Publishers, Inc., p. 286.

47. *North Africa Jews*, New York, 1906, p. 1.

48. *The Jews*, pp. 120 to 125; read also, G. Spiller: *Universal Races Congress*, p. 330, London, 1911.

Chapter 7

49. Aimé Césaire, *Discourse on Colonialism*, Paris, Présence Africaine, 1950, p. 20.

50. *Spiritual Letters*, as quoted by H. Gravand in *Visage African de l'Eglise*, Paris, 1961, p. 206.

51. Louis Vincent Thomas and René Luneau, *The African Land and Its Religions*, Paris, l'Harmattan, p. 128.

52. Louis Vincent Thomas and René Luneau, *The African Land and Its Religions*, ibid., p. 129.

53. Louis Vincent Thomas and Rene Luneau, *The African Land and Its Religions*, ibid., p. 130.

Chapter 8

54. Mary Lefkowitz, *Not Out Of Africa*, A New Republic Book, New York, NY, 1996.

55. Mary Lefkowitz, ibid., p. 122.

56. *The Great Political Theories,* Volume I, Section 1: The Greeks, Avon Discus Books, New York, NY, 1981, p. 23.

57. For more information on this topic, please read, *To Be Popular or Smart: The Black Peer Group,* by Jawanza Kunjufu, African American Images, Chicago, Illinois, 1988, pp. 11-15; *Ancient Egypt,* by John Kendrick, Book II, p. 55 and *History of Ancient Egypt,* Volume I, p. 234; Herodotus, *Book III,* p. 124; Sanford, *The Mediterranean World,* p. 562-570; Diogènes VIII 3; Philarch de Repugn, *Stoic* 2, p. 1089. Also, read *Stolen Legacy,* by George J. M. James, Julian Richardson Associates, Publishers, San Francisco, California, 1976; Cheikh Anta Diop, *The African Origin of Civilization: Myth or Reality,* Lawrence Hill Books, 1974; Cheikh Anta Diop, *Civilization or Barbarism,* Lawrence Hill Book, 1991.

58. *History Of Black Africa,* by Joseph Ki Zerbo, Paris, Hatier, 1978, p. 412.

59. General Charles De Gaulle, as quoted from, *Livre d'Histoire,* Volume III, IPAM, 1982, p. 129.

60. *L'Air des Négriers,* Paris, F. Alcan, 1931, p. 10. Also read Joseph Ki Zerbo, *History of Black Africa,* Paris, op. cit., p. 538.

Chapter 9
61. *The Bridge-Le Pont magazine,* Vol. I, No. 3, July 1995, p. 33.

62. Bruce Harris, in *The Bridge-Le Pont magazine*, ibid.

63. *Ebony magazine*, February 1993, p. 182.

64. Kevin Chappell, "How Blacks Invened Rock and Roll," in *Ebony magazine*, Volume LII, No. 3, January 1997, p. 52.

65. *Ebony*, ibid.

66. *Ebony*, ibid., p. 54.

67. *Ebony magazine*, "Remembering the Giants Of Music," Volume LI, No. 8, June 1996, p. 36.

68. *Ebony magazine*, ibid., p.37.

69. Joy Bennett Kinnon, "Why Black Male Stars Are Sizzling In Hollywood," in the magazine *EBONY*, A Johnson Publication, Volume LII, No 3, January 1997, p. 32.

Chapter 10

70. Late, Ron Brown, Secretary of Commerce in the Clinton administration 1992 to 1996, quoted from *People Who Have Made a Difference, Quotable Notables,* Nabisco Group, 1995.

71. *Africa Bank Balance*, Volume I, No 4, August-September 1995.

Chapter 11

72. *How Do Black Africans See Black Americans?* by Koffi David, in *The Bridge-Le Pont magazine*, October-November, 1995, p. 2.

73. Tyler Biggs, Gail R. Moody, Jan-Hendrik Van Leeuwen, and E. Diane White, *"Africa Can Compete: Export Opportunities and Challenges for Garments and Home Products in the U.S. Market,* The World Bank Discussion Paper, Africa Technical Department Series, August 1994.

Chapter 12

74. Jawanza Kunjufu, *To Be Popular or Smart: The Black Peer Group,* African American Images, Chicago, Illinois, 1988, p. 71.

NOTES

NOTES

NOTES

NOTES

NOTES

NOTES

NOTES

NOTES

NOTES